MASTERING MARKETING AGILITY

MASTERING MARKETING AGILITY

Transform Your Marketing Teams and Evolve Your Organization

ANDREA FRYREAR

Berrett-Koehler Publishers, Inc.

Berrett-Koehler Publishers, Inc.
1333 Broadway, Suite 1000
Oakland, CA 94612-1921
Tel: (510) 817-2277
Fax: (510) 817-2278
www.bkconnection.com.

ORDERING INFORMATION

Quantity sales. Special discounts are available on quantity purchases by corporations, associations, and others. For details, contact the Special Sales Department at the Berrett-Koehler address above.

Individual sales. Berrett-Koehler publications are available through most bookstores. They can also be ordered directly from Berrett-Koehler: Tel: (800) 929-2929; Fax: (802) 864-7626; www.bkconnection.com.

Orders for college textbook/course adoption use. Please contact Berrett-Koehler: Tel: (800) 929-2929; Fax: (802) 864-7626.

Distributed to the U.S. trade and internationally by Penguin Random House Publisher Services.

Printed in Canada

Berrett-Koehler books are printed on long-lasting acid-free paper. When it is available, we choose paper that has been manufactured by environmentally responsible processes. These may include using trees grown in sustainable forests, incorporating recycled paper, minimizing chlorine in bleaching, or recycling the energy produced at the paper mill.

Library of Congress Cataloging-in-Publication Data

Names: Fryrear, Andrea, author.
Title: Mastering marketing agility : transform your marketing teams and evolve your organization / Andrea Fryrear.
Description: First edition. | Oakland, CA : Berrett-Koehler Publishers, [2020] | Includes bibliographical references and index.
Identifiers: LCCN 2020002576 | ISBN 9781523090983 (paperback ; alk. paper) | ISBN 9781523089161 (pdf) | ISBN 9781523089178 (epub)
Subjects: LCSH: Marketing—Management.
Classification: LCC HF5415.13 .F79 2020 | DDC 658.8—dc23
LC record available at https://lccn.loc.gov/2020002576

First Edition

26 25 24 23 22 21 20 10 9 8 7 6 5 4 3 2 1

Interior design by Westchester Publishing Services
Cover design by Kim Scott, Bumpy Design

From A, for B, C, and D.

You are my people, and your amazingness makes everything I do, including this book, possible.

Contents

Foreword

Scott Brinker, Vice President of Platform Ecosystem, Hubspot

You're stressed, aren't you?

Okay, maybe not right at this *exact* moment. Maybe you're flipping through these pages at a bookstore with a soothing latte in your other hand. Or maybe you're sitting on the couch at home reading this with a glass of wine by your side. There are moments of calm for you, I hope.

But professionally, you work in marketing, and you've picked up a book on mastering marketing agility. So I'm going to go out on a limb and guess that you do regularly feel stressed in your job.

And why shouldn't you? Things keep changing throughout our industry. New demands keep flooding your inbox. The interconnections between your work and the rest of the organization keep expanding. The pace by which everything needs to run is constantly accelerating. Faster. And faster. And faster.

Whoa.

But don't panic. Take a deep breath, because I've got three pieces of good news for you.

First, you're not alone. Everyone in marketing today is affected by the same dizzying changes and quickening cycle speeds. Everyone feels the sensation of being overwhelmed. It's not you—it's the industry.

Second, the upside of working in this tumultuous, revolutionary period in marketing's history is that *the opportunity to make an impact has never been greater*. You are at the forefront of a whole new wave of marketing. If you're willing to experiment, learn, and adapt, you can unlock incredible value for your organization. And you can advance your career at a rate that people in other professions will admire and envy.

Third, you've got a terrific guidebook for navigating that opportunity in your hands. Andrea is one of the true pioneers of Agile marketing. She's wicked smart (I live in Boston, so that's the highest compliment we can give). She's amassed a ton of insight into Agile transformations from having taught, coached, and consulted for hundreds of marketing teams. The price of this book is a steal for tapping her wisdom.

But above all that, she has real empathy for the stress you've been feeling. She wants to show you a better way to harness these forces of speed and change, to turn them to your advantage.

Okay, so there's no guarantee that your job is going to become *completely* stress free after reading this. We can't do anything about that one drama-driven coworker in the lunchroom. However, if you embrace the recommendations that Andrea shares in the pages ahead, I'm quite certain that the balance between exhilaration and exhaustion in modern marketing will tip significantly in your favor.

There's really never been a better time to be a marketer.

Preface

This is a book about how.

It's not about why your company is in business, or why someone should choose you over your primary competitor. It isn't about whom you should target; it doesn't tell you the right segments to approach, or what your perfect persona might look like. It isn't about what marketing channels or tactics you need. It doesn't guide you to a perfect omnichannel strategy. It isn't here to help you blend artificial intelligence and machine learning into your marketing mix. It's about something greater than any of that.

Mastering Marketing Agility is about how to make your marketing activities—all of them—better.

Whatever your marketing looks like, the framework detailed here gets it flowing more smoothly. Whether you're business-to-business, business-to-consumer, business-to-government, an agency, or some beautiful hybrid of all of those, this book is here to make your marketing work predictable, productive, and sustainable.

Although I draw extensively from the Agile tradition to craft a new framework, I've learned the hard way that we can't build effective marketing operations based on one ideology. Over the last five years, I've used Agile marketing in many capacities—some amazing, some genuinely unpleasant. My major lesson across all those experiences has been a commitment to adaptation. Take my very first encounter with Agile marketing. I was a content marketer in a midsized software-as-a-service (SaaS) company, and my team was constantly getting crushed. We were supporting a *very* Agile software development team that released updates several times per week, and we just couldn't keep up.

One day, after scrambling around trying to get a suite of product announcement content updated to meet the development team's accelerated delivery schedule, I began to wonder why our marketers weren't following the same processes as this fast-paced team whose members were supposed to be our partners. If they were Agile, shouldn't we be? Otherwise, how could we ever hope to catch up? The following day I sat in my boss's office armed with the schedule for upcoming Scrum Master courses and a plan to overhaul our operations. He shrugged and agreed with my proposal. After all, it couldn't possibly be worse than the daily fire drills we currently handled.

A few weeks later I became a Certified Scrum Master, and shortly afterward our marketing department of seven became a Scrum team (we planned our work in two-week sprints, attempting to focus all our effort on only that high-value work). Then, about two sprints in, we realized things were breaking down. We never hit our sprint commitments, despite planning and estimating as carefully as we could at the start of each iteration. Turns out we had bolted some new practices on, but we hadn't done a very good job of changing mindsets. Sprint commitments aside, our executives still expected us to turn on a dime. Product development wasn't including us in their existing Agile process, and we weren't able to push back on urgent sales demands.

And so, like many Agile marketing teams have done, we pivoted.

We began incorporating more practices from Kanban (an Agile framework that emphasizes limited work in progress and doesn't use time-boxed sprints). Ultimately, we became a Scrumban team, blending aspects of both Scrum and Kanban into our own little hybrid that could roll with the punches of our daily professional lives. I didn't know it at the time, but that first Agile experience was a roadmap for everything that's come after. Team after team after team that I've coached has needed to hybridize, and they've struggled to make it happen.

We've all struggled because the frameworks we've been using weren't made for marketers. They were made for software developers.

Without a framework designed to work specifically for our profession, many Agile marketing teams begin with Scrum and flounder. The more resilient teams adapt; others abandon agility without giving it a real shot. And in the volatile, uncertain, complex, and ambiguous environment we inhabit, that's a major misstep. Agility is imperative—both inside and outside marketing. But to make it work for us, it needs to be tailored to our context.

Since that first foray into marketing agility, I've been unbelievably fortunate to spend several years training my fellow marketers—more than a thousand, across dozens of organizations and industries—in how to achieve agility. This book blends their voices and my experience with insights from some of the world's most amazing process thinkers, distilling it all into a new Agile framework built exclusively for marketing. That framework is called Rimarketing, after the Japanese concept of Shu Ha Ri (which I'll explain shortly).

In the coming chapters I touch on the need to create a robust marketing strategy to support agility, but this book isn't about crafting the perfect strategy.

This book includes a rabid focus on the customer, but it does not guide you through conducting customer interviews or market research.

I argue for informed decision making and process metrics, but I'm not here to tell you which key performance indicators (KPIs) to focus on.

Instead, this book is here to help your brilliant marketing ideas become reality by focusing on execution: where work gets—or fails to get—*done*. Foundational concepts help ensure success in execution, and in the early parts of the book you'll learn about them. But ultimately, this book assumes that you've got the strategy stuff down. We're not here to overhaul your marketing strategy.

This book is about transforming marketing operations.

We'll cover four topics, moving from general to specific, as we build the framework and execute your excellent ideas. (The titles of the parts are inspired by E. Jerome McCarthy's four P's of marketing: product, price, placement, and promotion.)

Part One: Principles

Every strong structure needs a firm foundation, so you'll first learn the seven principles that create the conditions necessary for an operation's marketing agility to thrive. You can start by implementing the processes and practices outlined in Parts Three and Four, but they won't reach their full potential without a commitment to these principles.

This chapter is particularly useful for marketing leaders, or those responsible for creating the cultural conditions inside a marketing department. You won't find tactical approaches here, but rather the core mindset shift that will lay a firm foundation for future changes at the team and process levels.

Part Two: People

Systems are made up of people, which is what makes systems tricky to manage. You need to understand how to support real humans as they execute the complex knowledge work of modern marketing, and this chapter will help you do that. Most important, here you'll discover the perils of project-based teams (and the Agile approach that offers an antidote).

Current marketing leaders, along with anybody who hopes to lead marketing teams, will find impactful insights here. Individual contributors who don't manage anyone will learn how to best position themselves for success inside an Agile marketing system.

Part Three: Processes

This part shows you how to set up marketing processes optimized for flow, predictability, and sustainability. Merely moving at top speed all the time won't cut it; we need a system that connects daily work, strategic objectives, and customer needs, all while supporting the people within the system.

All marketers will find something to implement here. You'll learn ways to restructure teams for greater productivity, find out how to collaborate more effectively with other groups, and generally organize your workflow to get more done in less time (you know . . . agility).

Part Four: Practices

The lion's share of the book dives deep into the recurring practices of Rimarketing because they embody some of the most fundamental shifts in execution for many marketers. You'll see how to connect strategic perspectives with ongoing activities, how to visualize work, when to meet and what to talk about, how to identify and eliminate bottlenecks, and more.

Team leaders and individual contributors: this section is for you. Improve productivity, unblock workflows, identify underperformers—your process problems are tackled here. For marketing executives overseeing an Agile transformation in their organization, this section may sound too "in the weeds." But even you will learn productivity hacks that you probably haven't seen anywhere else.

Why Rimarketing?

We can't go farther without pausing to unpack the name of the framework whose components make up this volume. The "Ri" in "Rimarketing" comes from the concept of Shu Ha Ri, a Japanese phrase that tracks the progression, in any area of skill, from novice to master.

We begin in the Shu phase. We learn and follow the rules. We color inside the lines, and we do what experts tell us to do. We haven't yet mastered the fundamentals of the process, so we can't yet make intelligent adjustments to it.

Eventually, at our own pace, we advance from Shu into the Ha phase. We have just enough expertise to bend the rules a little, to get creative. Our actions still fall squarely within the limits of traditional practices, but we're learning to flex and adapt those practices.

We arrive ultimately at Ri, the phase of creation and innovation. While our activities still connect to, and are recognizable as, the practices used in Shu and Ha, in the Ri phase we invent and create.

The world contains many examples of this evolutionary process, but for my money nothing drives it home quite like the big dance scene at Rydell High in the movie *Grease*. A national dance show has chosen Rydell as the site of its contest, and the students perform their best moves in an attempt to win stardom and glory.

One couple, Doody and Frenchy, are firmly in the Shu phase. Doody can barely follow the prescribed steps of a traditional waltz. "Doody, can't you at least turn me around or something?" Frenchy pleads, as Doody marches woodenly across the gym floor holding her stiffly in his arms. "Be quiet, French. I'm tryin' to count." Shu phase all the way.

Next, during the Hand Jive, lots of kids demonstrate their attainment of the Ha level. Hand Jive has a set of prescribed motions, and many of the couples expand on that foundation. Rather than merely clapping, tapping fists on top of each other, and jerking thumbs over their shoulders, they add moves. Staying with the beat, following the prescribed pattern of executing each move twice, the more experienced dancers comfortably experiment within the framework of the dance.

The camera then moves to Danny and Sandy, the romantic leads (played by John Travolta and Olivia Newton-John). Danny and Sandy also move in rhythm, but beyond that they make up everything as they go along, dancing far more inventively than the other couples. They play off each other's moves, leading and following one another to create a unique series of steps for each song. Like all Ri dancers, they operate creatively and effectively within the boundaries of their given dance tradition. Their actions are built on the fundamentals they learned in the Shu stage, but they look nothing like those basic steps. They've evolved far beyond "I'm tryin' to count." They are in Ri, flowing, adapting, experimenting, always in the moment, always creating.

Rimarketing is Agile marketing at the Ri level. I didn't want to call the framework simply "Agile marketing," although technically I suppose that moniker would be accurate. I've spent the last five years of my professional life exploring Agile marketing and training others to do the same, and while I still believe deeply in the power of that approach, this book outlines something distinct from the way Agile marketing has been practiced until now.

Agile marketing, at first, was very much a Shu practice for everyone. The Agile Marketing Manifesto, drawing heavily on the original Agile Manifesto for Software Development, was drafted in 2011. Because few people had used Agile concepts in marketing, we took the existing Agile frameworks as they were written and applied them to our own work. This meant using Scrum, because Scrum was the most widely known and because training on its practices was the most readily available.

As we gained experience and moved Agile marketing into the Ha stage, it evolved. Late in 2016, three leaders—Jim Ewel, Yuval Yeret, and I—wrote the curriculum for the first internationally recognized certification in Agile marketing. The International Consortium for Agile (ICAgile) was the certifying body, and its framework-agnostic approach helped to catalyze the shift away from our early attempts to force-fit Scrum onto marketing work and toward hybrid approaches. The certification requires trainers to know both iteration-based and flow-based frameworks (typically Scrum and Kanban, respectively); as a result, new Agile marketing practitioners have a broad understanding, from the jump, of what Agile can do.

A growing force of accredited trainers now delivers this certification; many Agile teams are poised to enter the Ha stage and experiment inside existing Agile frameworks. Figure 1 illustrates the high percentage of Agile marketing teams using a hybrid approach in 2019, a sure sign of the Ha stage in action.

Amazing though all of this might be, we live still in a Ha stage; we are constrained by the boundaries of existing frameworks. Rimarketing aims to impel marketing's ascent to its own unique version of agility.

One way to think of Rimarketing's place in the Agile pantheon is to compare it to newer Agile scaling frameworks, such as SAFe (Scaled Agile Framework; scaledagile.com), LeSS (Large Scale Scrum; less.works), and Scrum@Scale (scrumatscale.com). These processes are considerably newer than the core Agile frameworks of Kanban and Scrum, but they've emerged out of necessity as Agile software development has expanded to encompass complex enterprise departments rather than a couple of fast-moving teams of developers.

As you'll soon see, Rimarketing, while rooted in the Agile tradition, likewise brings something new and unique. It's the marriage of

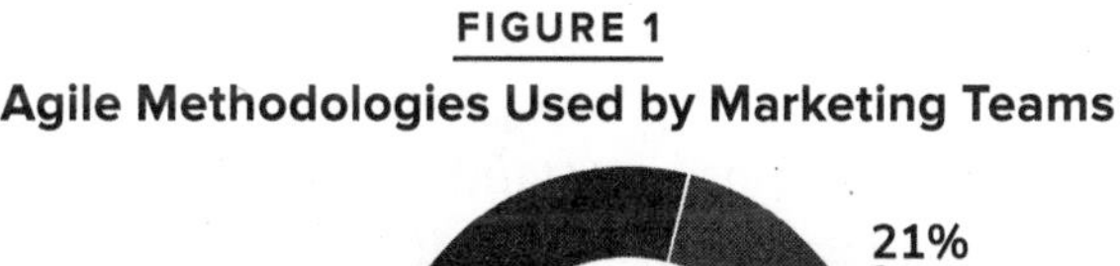

FIGURE 1

Agile Methodologies Used by Marketing Teams

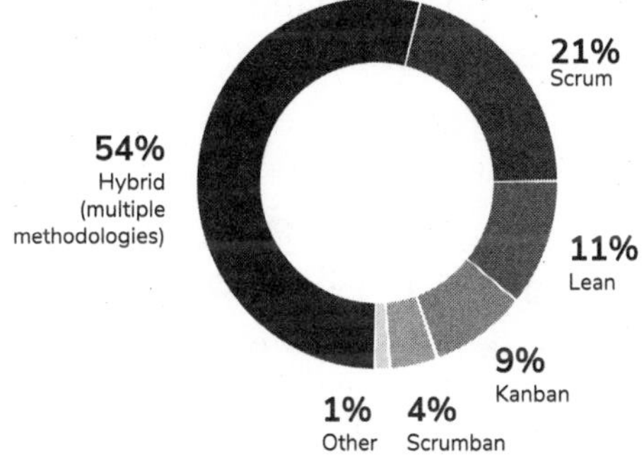

Source: State of Agile Marketing Report 2019, AgileSherpas and CoSchedule.

agility and marketing in a way that simply hasn't been available before. Like scaling frameworks, it's emerging out of necessity. Marketing agility can't succeed if it's a carbon copy of Agile software development. We need our own approach. After years of working side by side with my fellow marketers, I believe Rimarketing is our best approach for moving forward. It's absolutely part of the Agile tradition, but it involves a unique implementation designed to adapt Agile values to the marketing profession.

Before we launch into exploring the framework itself, we need to take a slight detour to talk about the imperiled marketing executive, the chief marketing officer (CMO), and where they fit in the Rimarketing revolution.

Extending the CMO Lifespan

When a CMO is hired, somewhere an hourglass flips over. Grains of sand begin plummeting from the upper half, piling up inexorably in the bottom until time runs out and the CMO is politely asked to leave. It's a grim picture, and it turns out the hourglass isn't even very big compared to those measuring out the lifespan of other executives. Recent data from the executive placement firm Korn Ferry revealed an average tenure of 3 years for CMOs, 2.3 years less than for the C-suite in aggregate (see Figure 2).

While brutal, this high rate of churn isn't completely surprising to those of us who have spent much time (more than three years, if the data are accurate) in the marketing profession.

Here's how it often goes: a CMO gets hired, then spends sixty to ninety days listening and learning (and stressing out a whole department's worth of people by meeting with them one on one). Then

FIGURE 2

Average CMO Tenure Is Only 3 Years

Rimarketing Framework® AgileSherpas.

they unveil their new Marketing Vision, complete with all caps, a huge PowerPoint presentation, and much fanfare. Chances are they embark on a brand update or a website refresh early on—sometimes even both. Although there's technically nothing wrong with either of those tactics if the timing and objectives are right, they represent some of the most amorphous marketing projects out there. It's often difficult to pin down thorny questions like

- When are they done? Who decides?
- How do we measure the impact?
- Whose approval is necessary and at which stage?
- How long should we delay if this approval isn't forthcoming?

Both strategies also commonly fall prey to scope creep, in which the original plan balloons and takes months longer than anticipated (at least in a non-Agile environment). Everyone has an opinion about branding and websites, which can mean that rounds of review and revision may drag on for months. Both are also highly subjective. It's impossible to decide if a particular shade of blue makes us feel hopeful or optimistic, yet we'll spend hours debating such unprovable questions.

Consequently, early CMO efforts take a *really* long time to get done, and even longer to start showing quantifiable results. Factor in the typical inability to prove an actual return on investment (ROI) for these activities, and it's no wonder that inevitable collapse imperils CMOs everywhere.

With the clock ticking loudly in their ears, and the website update barely launched, CMOs start getting nervous at around the two-year mark. They're running low on sand in their hourglass, and they can feel it. Then the poor decision making begins in earnest. Their early efforts to shore up brand identity and push for long-term vision aren't delivering, at least not in a way they can prove to the CFO, so they start to optimize for the near term. This newly myopic perspective is often compounded by the board and the CEO, who have most likely been surreptitiously looking at quarterly results all along but have been giving the CMO "some wiggle room" during their early months.

As the flailing continues, tactical quick wins get prioritized over long-term strategy. In some cases, this flurry of activity will buy the

CMO time, especially if they can growth hack their way to a few significant flashy outcomes. But eventually the tactic well runs dry, the numbers flatten out, and the CMO moves along.

If you're a CMO or vice president who'd like to write a different ending for yourself, this book provides you with the roadmap you need. When you get hired and the hourglass gets flipped, it could be counting down to your first big win instead of your eventual demise.

This alternative ending is valuable not just for the CMOs themselves and the marketers who suffer from whiplash trying to jump from one boss to another. It also reverses the impact on the company of the revolving door of CMOs. Deloitte reports, "One portfolio analysis shows that stocks of companies where a CMO is part of the top management team—often signaling a corporate-wide, customer-centric focus—netted shareholders significantly higher long-term returns than portfolios lacking CMO emphasis. These results were magnified for organizations that had a relatively high R&D and advertising spend."[1]

Ultimately, CMO churn is bad for everyone. It's bad for the CMOs themselves, bad for the teams they lead, bad for the organizations they work for, and bad for the audiences who are exposed to the haphazard marketing their teams generate. Fortunately, by shortening launch times and emphasizing continuous delivery of customer value, the Rimarketing system outlined in this book not only halts this vicious cycle; it turns marketing into a value-adding, customer-centric hub of excellence helmed by a trusted executive who represents the customer's voice.

Rimarketing is designed to revamp and realign operations across the marketing function, meaning that CMOs can deliver—and prove—their value early and often. And by "early" I mean within six months, not three years. The practices outlined here will help you make every single marketing item that flows through your organization work better, be of higher quality, and be more likely to pro-

---

1. Diana O'Brien, Timothy Murphy, and Jennifer Veenstra. "Redefining the CMO." *Deloitte Review*, Issue 22, January 22, 2018. https://www2.deloitte.com/us/en/insights/deloitte-review/issue-22/redefining-the-role-of-the-cmo-chief-marketing-officer.html.

duce quantifiable impact. No need to wait months (or years) for the traditional Big Bang approach to be completed and start to yield results; by creating minimum viable campaigns with cross-functional teams and iterating based on incoming data, you'll start to see, feel, and prove your worth much faster.

Executives and marketing leaders: implement the operational changes outlined in the following pages, and turn your next gig into the one that makes a difference.

PART 1

PRINCIPLES
The Fertile Soil of Marketing Agility

> But a war, a strike for a principle is never a mistake, never odious, never unwise on the part of those who contend for the principle, for the right, for the truth.
>
> ANONYMOUS, *THE STATION AGENT*, JANUARY 1894

I'LL BE THE FIRST to admit, the detailed processes and practices that form the latter part of this book are a little like the sleek exterior of a sports car. They're what everybody sees, the things that elicit "oohs" and "aahs" from passersby.

But without a foundation, even the shiniest surface fades. A snazzy sports car with a crappy engine is a major disappointment. Likewise, without shared principles acting as a driving force, even the best-intentioned process stands little chance of lasting success. So with these principles, you'll build the engine of your Rimarketing vehicle.

Rimarketing is based on the seven principles summarized below. They're not lifted directly from the Agile Manifesto or the Scrum Guide, but if you know Agile, you'll recognize some themes. Here, like everything in these pages, they're tailored to marketing's needs.

1. **Customer Focus:** All members of the marketing organization, from the CMO to the brand new intern, understand and value customers, defined as the external audience for marketing messages, the internal customers and stakeholders, and all who have bought (or will buy) something.
2. **Radical Transparency:** Put simply, information is shared. Teams know what's going on with their members and with

other teams. They know the long-term direction of the company, and they know whether the milestones to those objectives are being met. Information hoarding, at the executive or individual level, does not exist in Rimarketing.

3. **Continuous Improvement:** Things can always be better. Even if we're far from where we want to be, we willingly take steps, short and long, to reach our goal. Rimarketing processes harness the power of forward momentum.
4. **Adaptability:** Planning is important; plans, less so. We acknowledge and embrace changing conditions, folding them, when appropriate, into planning and execution.
5. **Trust:** Teams must trust the direction of senior leaders, leaders must trust their teams to do great work, and team members must trust one another to support their shared goals. Outside the marketing organization, customers must trust in the ethics of the marketers who are communicating with them. Internal customers and stakeholders must also trust marketing to deliver on its commitments.
6. **Bias toward Action:** Do something, even if it might be wrong. Although we prefer to take action based on long experience and great data, we also prefer acting on incomplete information over waiting until we have an overwhelming body of evidence.
7. **Courage:** Rimarketing calls on its members to make hard choices regularly. Whether it's advocating for the customer, pointing out a process flaw, or calling out colleagues on poor behavior, everyone needs the courage to do the right thing.

Principle 1: Customer Focus

As used here, "customer" includes many who have not bought and some who may never buy. A marketing team's customers fall into three main categories, and some teams may serve more than one of them:

- **Internal customers:** An organization has lots of people—those in sales, product development, customer service, user experience, and even other marketing functions—who need things from the marketing team. Although these internal groups probably aren't a firm's sole customers, a Rimarketing team must still serve them and balance their needs against those of paying customers.
- **Content marketing consumers:** With the rise of content marketing since the early part of the twenty-first century, most marketing groups direct the bulk of their time and resources to cultivating a relationship with an audience. The team hopes these people will become customers, and they continuously create and give away valuable content for them to that end.
- **Traditional customers:** A Rimarketing team, of course, attends also to those who buy what the organization sells.

Any team activity must clearly serve at least one of these customers. Only a request with a clear customer connection makes it into the workflow. (We'll look more closely at the value of saying no from a process perspective later.) The Rimarketing team knows its customers intimately, and it pushes back hard against taking on work that doesn't serve them.

Of course, one customer's needs may conflict with another's. A sales representative may want us to drop everything this week to create custom marketing materials for a high-dollar prospect call, and we've planned to spend the week creating new content resources for our pre-purchase audience. Sales is an internal customer, and email subscribers and social media followers who consume our content are also customers. What do we do?

Here, process kicks in, putting the team's leadership in contact with the requesting sales rep so that leadership can evaluate the request against the team's existing commitments. Since understanding each customer is central to the customer-focus principle, we—our team and its leaders—must prioritize based on what we know about each customer.

This level of understanding requires effort. Taking time to explore the needs of customers up front is vital, but we don't want the Rimarketing process stalled by a need to learn the basics about our customers so that we can make a time-sensitive prioritization call.

Getting to Know Your Customers

Per the sixth Rimarketing principle, we have a bias toward action, even in our customer exploration. We don't want to spend months on persona creation when we can use lightweight tools to get to know them. This approach enables us to move quickly from an informed position, while understanding that our knowledge is basic and incomplete. Finally, we balance all the Agile exploration tools that we'll discuss here against the need to hold, whenever possible, conversations with real customers.

And by "conversations" I don't mean looking at their lead score in your customer-relations management (CRM) software, or reviewing segment behavior in your website analytics. I mean talking with actual people who represent your customer segments. Some of the tools described below focus these conversations on actionable takeaways; others help you document an imaginary dialogue with a customer you already know well. But never assume that a canvas or a persona is a replacement for regular interaction with the people you want to reach.

Minimum Viable Persona

The first customer centricity tool we'll explore is the Minimum Viable Persona. Based on the Minimum Viable Product concept popularized by Eric Ries's *Lean Startup*, this approach to audience categorization aims to collect the minimum amount of information necessary to begin communicating effectively with a group.

Traditional marketing teams are prone to spending many months and thousands of dollars on crafting a perfect, data-centric persona. They conduct lengthy surveys, slice and dice the data dozens of ways, follow up with in-person interviews, and refine it all into a beautiful document like the one shown in Figure 3.

Don't get me wrong; personas are valuable components of modern marketing. I do not advocate their elimination. What I'm arguing for is something more lightweight, more Agile.

FIGURE 3

Traditional Persona Diagram

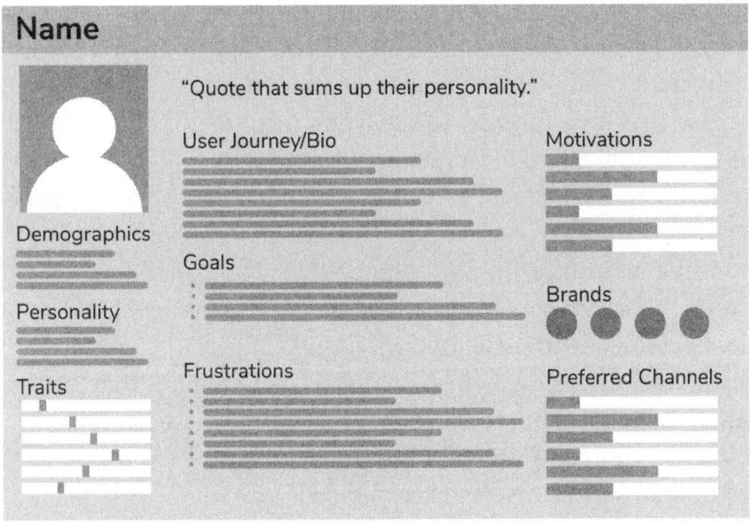

Source: Author.

Like a Minimum Viable Product, a Minimum Viable Persona assumes that you can't know everything up front, no matter how many surveys you distribute or how many customer interviews you conduct. Knowledge gaps remain.

Furthermore, you uncover the most actionable and important pieces of information about your audience in the earliest parts of your research. Later efforts serve as validation for early insights; they rarely reveal anything new. If we map the value we derive on persona creation against the time it takes us to obtain it, we see diminishing returns.

Chances are that the Pareto Principle, also known as the 80/20 rule, is at play here. This mathematical principle tells us that the relationship between most things follows an 80/20 split. Eighty percent of the value from our persona efforts, for instance, comes from just 20 percent of the work.

So we need to get that revelatory, actionable information quickly. We want to accomplish that super valuable 20 percent of the work first; then we can decide whether to pursue the remaining 80 percent.

(Because it forms a foundational idea of Rimarketing, this principle recurs throughout the book: we identify and execute first those activities that provide a disproportionately large amount of value.) One way to do this is to tap into internal knowledge about our customer base(s), using an exercise called Four Objects.[1]

To use this tool, have someone who's intimately acquainted with your target audience collect four physical objects that provide insight into the customer's ideas, behavior, and personality. For instance, if you're a B2C marketer selling athletic shoes to people who are new to running, your four objects might be (1) a stack of books on basic running topics, (2) screen shots of podcasts on living a healthy lifestyle, (3) athletic-style headphones, and (4) medals and bibs from marathons. Bonus points if you can find a member of that audience segment to help collect these items. Preferably these components of the person's personality will intersect with your own product, service, or marketing messaging, but you can work with what you have.

Next, gather a group who'll be responsible for communicating with this audience member. Most likely you'll have marketing, sales, and customer experience/success/service in the room; you may also want to bring in executives and other leaders, but be aware that their presence might decrease brainstorming potential.

Finally, have everyone take a look at the objects and fill out the Minimum Viable Persona Canvas depicted in Figure 4. (You can find a downloadable version at MasteringMarketingAgility.com.)

You're looking for a way to tap into the knowledge of the group and get consensus around the following:

- core traits of the audience that will form the foundation of your marketing messaging for them
- several hypotheses that can be tested with marketing or sales efforts—that is, ideas that some people believe are true but that lack consensus from the internal focus group

1. Hat tip to John Lane (@johnvlane on Twitter), who first introduced me to this concept.

FIGURE 4

Minimum Viable Persona Canvas

Industry	Demographics	Q/A
Interests	Communication Preferences	

Adapted from a canvas by Centerline Digital.

You can also supplement your on-the-ground persona work with secondary data from the internet. Identify a representative from your audience segment about whom you already have insights through your existing tools. (Even a simple Google Analytics review works here, but it's more effective to pull a record from your CRM and review real activity.) What pages do they visit on your site? How do they behave on social media? What words do they use when talking about their problems and solutions? What content do they share and respond to?

Use the answers to some of these questions to resolve discrepancies that emerge during your Persona Canvas creation. Again, you're looking for just enough information to get started, so don't burn a week on this investigation. This is, as discussed, a Minimum Viable Persona, not the final product. What do I mean by these terms?

- It's "Minimum" in that we've collected the smallest amount of information possible to enable future action.
- It's "Viable" because it's a functional, stand-alone document—but by no means the end of the process.

As we learn more about this customer *by communicating with them*, we expand and update our canvas. Communication here may take place through conversations, email exchanges, or phone calls, or it may occur through marketing channels. The level of engagement this person displays with our marketing collateral tells us how accurately we've characterized them. We document the answers to our initial questions and hypotheses and use the new information to adjust how we communicate with this audience segment.

We expand on our Minimum Viable Persona, adding value and functionality until, ultimately, it resembles the beautifully crafted persona document shown in Figure 3. And rather than sit while we spent months creating a perfect piece of research, we connect with our audience and regularly learn about them.

Value Proposition Canvas

Once we know more about who we're communicating with, we then make sure that we solve their problems with our marketing. We do this by conducting a handful of customer interviews, discussing with them their previous problems and current solutions. Our goal here is to align our work with what our customers want, rather than with what we imagine they want.

Take fifteen or twenty minutes to interview a few customers, and you'll be amazed at what you learn. Use the following questions to guide the interview, letting the conversation flow easily. Do not press to have all your questions answered!

1. **Triggering Event:** What are the conditions that created a desire for change? What's hard about _______?
2. **Desired Outcome:** How was success first defined? If you previously experienced success, what was it like?
3. **Old Solution:** What existing solution (if any) is already in place?
4. **Consideration Set:** What alternative solutions will be/have been considered?
5. **New Solution:** What new solution was selected last time you were in this situation?
6. **Inertia:** What habits/anxieties/behaviors hold you back from switching to the new solution?
7. **Friction:** What habits/anxieties/behaviors got in the way during the use of the new solution?

8. **Actual Outcome:** Was the job done? Was it done well? How could it be better?
9. **Next Summit:** What are you going to do next?

If that format seems heavy, you can always just ask, "What was hard about the last time you [did the thing we're hoping to help you do]?" If you listen closely, what you discover may be surprising.

Remember that your customers might not always be external; don't be afraid to try this same thing with your internal customers.

Once you've conducted the initial interview, use your notes to complete the right side of the Value Proposition Canvas shown in Figure 5. You can also download a blank version at MasteringMarketingAgility.com.

As illustrated, you want to split your insights into three sections:

1. Gains
2. Pains
3. Jobs to be done

This last insight comes from product development, where feature creep can be avoided by aligning the group around a focus on what the customer wants the product to do. For instance, we might say that as marketers we hire email-marketing software to send emails to the right people at the right time so that we don't have to do it manually.

FIGURE 5

Value Proposition Canvas

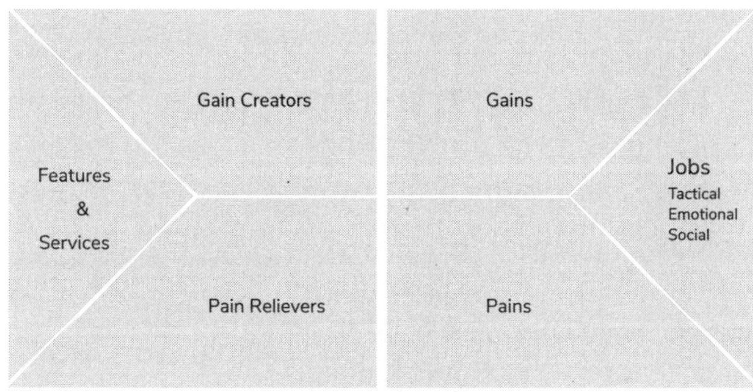

Canvas based on original by Alexander Osterwalder.

Given that point of view, people developing email marketing software can focus on building things that help us do those jobs. They can create all kinds of spam or GDPR compliance features, or make it dead simple to design stunning emails, but if those aren't the jobs we want this tool to do for us, we don't buy the product based on those features.

Similarly, we want to create marketing materials that solve the problems our audiences face. They have jobs to do; we want to be the ones they choose to help them.

Continuing with our email automation example, the marketing team for this tool would want to focus on creating collateral that helps marketers do the identified jobs, for example:

- Send to the right people.
- Send at the right time.
- Avoid manual work.

Notice that the canvas identifies three kinds of jobs: tactical, emotional (or psychological), and social. As marketers, we must focus on differentiating among these because people hire our marketing to accomplish tasks across this spectrum, especially when it comes to sharing content.

Emotional tasks make us feel or think a certain way. If I can send more emails and all of them get higher levels of engagement, I feel successful at my job. I might also feel less overwhelmed by the volume of emails I have to create by hand. The marketers for the email automation tool can build on that psychological task in their messaging and campaigns.

Social jobs are more about how activities make us look to people around us. For marketing this is most relevant to things like social media shares and email forwards. When customers, prospects, or audience members share something we've created, what message are they sending to their followers? Do they look smart for being up on the latest research? Are they clever for sending around a funny email-related meme? Sometimes we need to lean into the social tasks and away from the more serious tactical ones.

That can be hard to do, because tactical jobs are the ones we really like to talk about. These are the ways our features and benefits make customers' lives easier. That's a tried-and-true marketing conversation, and it's one we want to have *all the time*. There are certainly times when tactical tasks should be the focus of our marketing, but even then it should be about what a customer would hire our product, service, or marketing collateral to do for them. It's their job to be done, and we're here to help. They're the hero of the story; we're the supporting character.

Once we've completed the right side of the canvas and identified these areas of opportunity, we can start designing actual marketing activities to meet those needs. Now's the time to talk channels and tactics, all with the focus on the items collected on the canvas. This helps us stay attuned to the audience, rather than getting lost in great ideas for cool new campaigns that may or may not add value.

Principle 2: Radical Transparency

The second Rimarketing principle involves a willingness to be open about all aspects of a process. Said another way, it's a commitment to providing visibility into everything you do in a way that demands very little work by your team or an outside observer.

Information hoarding—at any level, by anyone—does not happen in Rimarketing. Teams know what's going on with their own members and with other teams. They also know the long-term direction of the company and whether interim goals are being met.

Radical transparency as a concept was first introduced by Ray Dalio in the early 1990s. He explained it this way in a recent interview: "When I say I believe in radical truth and radical transparency, all I mean is we take things that ordinarily people would hide and we put them on the table—particularly mistakes, problems, and weaknesses—and we look at them together."[2]

---

2. Henry Blodget, "In a Revealing Interview with Henry Blodget, Ray Dalio Offers a Radical Solution to the Threat of 'Fake News' and Details Life Inside Bridgewater," *BusinessInsider*, January 7, 2017, https://www.businessinsider.com/ray-dalio-interview-henry-blodget-1-2017.

If you've built a workflow but it's in a password-protected document, or in a tool that requires a lengthy account creation, or on a wall in a part of the building that nobody visits, you might be adhering to the letter of this principle, but you're missing the spirit. Likewise, if you're a leader who created a yearly vision, complete with high-level objectives, and you buried it on slide 137 in a deck that you emailed on a Friday afternoon, you're not *really* practicing radical transparency.

Again, information hoarding cannot happen if Rimarketing is to thrive. Each member of every marketing team needs to be comfortable sharing the details of their work, and that includes leaders.

The knee-jerk reaction to this kind of blanket statement can be that it's dangerous to give everyone access to everything; surely we need to keep some things under wraps. Or perhaps information overload will burden our teams, or excessive sharing will distract them from getting their day-to-day work done.

There's certainly a limit to openness, beyond which sharing becomes hazardous to a company's productivity and financial health. I'm not asking you to cross any ethical lines in the pursuit of radical transparency. What I *am* trying to avoid is a situation like the one I recently encountered in which a CMO declined to join her team for a training session because she didn't want them to see her learning. Despite Agile marketing being a completely new operating model for the whole department, this executive wanted to appear fully informed from day one.

Although leaders' roles in an Agile environment are unique (we often train them on specific leadership topics in a separate session), the attitude conveyed in this small interaction is troubling. It runs directly counter to transparency; it's more concerned with maintaining appearances than with sharing an experience.

Consider Buffer, a SaaS company that has for years practiced radical transparency across the enterprise. They state their value as "Default to Transparency," and they've devoted an entire section of their website to it (https://buffer.com/transparency).

You'll find some typical things on that list, such as a product roadmap and their corporate values. Not typically, you'll also find the salaries for every employee, an editorial calendar showing all upcoming content ideas, and a real-time revenue dashboard. Before embracing oversharing, Buffer wasn't making many waves. They were another startup in a sea of martech vendors. As soon as they defaulted to transparency, they distinguished their brand and became a sought-after employer and a trusted name among marketing tools.

New data explain Buffer's success. A 2011 experiment comparing consumer valuation of websites that provided operational transparency—in this case by revealing more detail about what their software was doing (searching databases, collecting results, analyzing responses)—showed that more transparency created a perception of more value. According to Ryan Buell and Michael Norton, the authors of the study, this type of operational transparency "provides cues for consumers to better understand how the quantity of work being conducted translates into how hard the company is working for them."[3]

Those of us in marketing can likewise increase our perceived value, internally and externally, by being radically transparent about what we do. We can provide internal partners with a detailed, prioritized list of upcoming work through the use of a queue (more on this in Parts Three and Four). And like Buffer does, we can let our external audiences know what content we're thinking about sharing with them by making available our editorial calendar and publishing schedule. Both practices enhance marketing's perceived value by providing a radical change from a combative corporate culture and a way to offset the decline in consumer trust of brands, both of which plague the marketing profession.

Workfront's 2016 State of Marketing Work discovered that 98 percent of marketers experience conflict with other teams.[4] We've

---

3. Ryan W. Buell and Michael I. Norton, "The Labor Illusion: How Operational Transparency Increases Perceived Value," *Management Science* 57, no. 9 (September 2011), https://studylib.net/doc/10493918/management-science.

4. "The US State of Marketing Work Report, 2016–2017," https://www.workfront.com/sites/default/files/resource/file_pdf/2018-05/2016-17-u-s-state-of-marketing-work-report.pdf.

got a lot of fences to mend. Whether those conflicts arise because marketing fails to hit deadlines, fails to align on shared objectives, or simply leaves other teams in the dark, radical transparency improves marketing teams' relationships with other groups.

When it comes to our external customers (remember, these may include regular customers as well as the audience for our content who haven't yet purchased anything from us), marketers could use a shot of perceived value as well. Marketing work is inextricably linked with brand value and associations, so if the brand suffers a setback, our work becomes harder. This is becoming increasingly common, as trust in brands across the board has declined for the past decade and a half.

According to Young and Rubicam's Brand Asset Valuator, adult consumers in the United States simply don't trust brands as much as they used to. Trust, running at 44 percent in 2001, sat at 18 percent in 2017.[5] Radical transparency in marketing can help reverse this trend too.

Although useful and valuable, these relationship-focused benefits are often secondary. The importance of radical transparency for Rimarketing lies primarily in its ability to bring to the surface impediments and improvements in process, remove misunderstandings, and enhance collaboration at all levels of the marketing function.

It is vital to avoid confusing radical transparency with excessive oversight. As we'll see in Part Two, "People," Rimarketing demands trust and empowerment of employees. In a 2014 *Harvard Business Review* article, Ethan Bernstein argues, "For all that transparency does to drive out wasteful practices and promote collaboration and shared learning, too much of it can trigger distortions of fact and counterproductive inhibitions."[6] After conducting field research of his own and reviewing existing literature, Bernstein found a disconcerting connection between secrecy and observation. When they were monitored constantly, employees responded with instinctive se-

5. Carolyn Hanuschek, "The Decline of Trust," *BAV Group, Brands and Culture*. October 9, 2017, https://www.bavgroup.com/brands-culture/decline-trust.
6. Ethan Bernstein. "The Transparency Trap," *Harvard Business Review*, October 2014, https://hbr.org/2014/10/the-transparency-trap.

crecy. Bernstein found that "individuals and groups routinely wasted significant resources in an effort to conceal beneficial activities, because they believed that bosses, peers, and external observers who might see them would have 'no idea' how to 'properly understand' them." This is, in fact, an argument in favor of radical transparency across the organization, not just at the team or individual level. When everyone shares naturally, you don't need Orwellian tactics.

Employee productivity declines when people feel constantly monitored, so it is important to make sure that transparency is freely practiced by all members of the marketing team rather than rigidly enforced by marketing leadership. Creating this balance requires a nuanced understanding of human behavior and biases, and it requires that leadership be willing to walk a fine line in the service of achieving outstanding results.

Principle 3: Continuous Improvement

As we'll learn in later parts of the book, Rimarketing focuses on processes and practices that yield benefits early in the transformation process. While these early wins might tempt us to sit back and hit pause on our operational efforts, the benefits continue only as long as we're committed to long-term, continuous improvement.

Groups looking to overhaul their operations typically pass a tipping point, a place where the discomfort and inconvenience of change is less than the pain and inefficiency of their current ways of working. The danger of making simple, quick adjustments is that we may soon find ourselves back, just barely, on the other side of that tipping point. We haven't created lasting solutions to our process problems; we've merely alleviated the most acute pain points.

To produce all the benefits of agility that Rimarketing offers, the approach to improvement must be continuous, not a one-and-done item on a checklist. We're looking to change operations at their core; only this deep level of evolution delivers lasting innovation and consistent, sustainable, valuable marketing work.

Think of it as an evolution that begins with a revolution. You can do some things right away—especially if your existing processes are in a particularly dismal state—to get you faster, better marketing. That's the revolution—the early changes that yield a big impact. But the ongoing, continuous evolution of the way you plan and design campaigns, structure your teams, hire new talent, and respond to success and failure is what alters your marketing team's DNA. This kind of change is what creates innovation and extraordinary achievement, and this kind of change is what Rimarketing delivers over time.

Like most of the seven principles, continuous improvement applies at all levels of an organization. Individuals, teams, and leaders must commit to climbing the ladder of progress. Let's consider each of these groups in turn.

Individual marketers commit to improving their skills and broadening their capabilities to become cross-functional members of the Rimarketing organization. Cross-functional (T-shaped) marketers have a broad foundational knowledge of marketing, enabling them to contribute to a wide variety of work (see Figure 6).

We'll discuss more ways to develop or hire such people; at the moment, simply note that all marketers must know what their crossbar (the top of the T) looks like now, and what it must look like for them to be most effective. They must have a plan for shoring up weak spots

FIGURE 6

T-Shaped Marketers

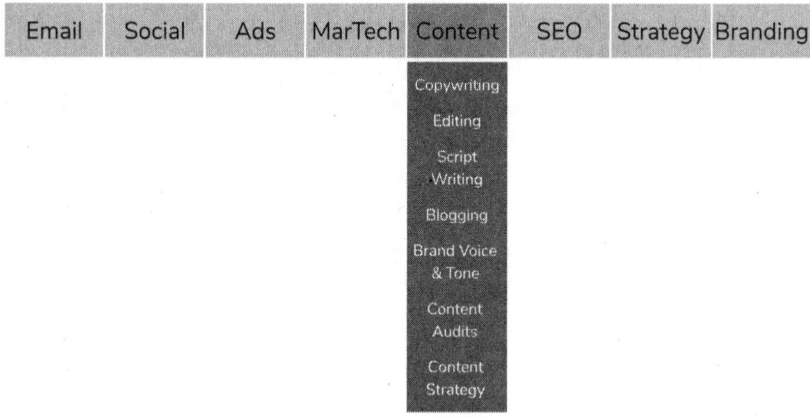

Rimarketing Framework® AgileSherpas.

FIGURE 7

Stages of Team Development

Forming
- Independent behaviors by team members
- Focused on themselves
- Unclear on objectives
- No collaboration or cooperation

Storming
- Form opinions of others on team
- Challenge behavior of other team members
- Some collaborative behavior
- No team norms

Norming
- Shared purpose emerges
- Relationship has increased
- Shared responsibility
- Greater tolerance of other team members
- Norms are established

Performing
- Team is self-organizing and can make decisions
- Full engagement of team members
- Embrace differences with higher empathy
- Delivering valuable results

Adapted from Stages of Team Development by Bruce Tuckman.

and increasing their subject-matter expertise. People who chafe against self-improvement may find this challenging; it's up to the team to decide whether to accept any member who can't (or won't) formally embrace the principle of continuous improvement.

Speaking of teams: in a good Rimarketing implementation, these persistent groups strive to achieve high-performing status, working through the issues that arise in the early days of the team's formation rather than sweeping them under a rug (see Figure 7).

You've probably encountered these four phases before; they were originally outlined by educational psychologist Bruce Tuckman back in 1965 in his article "Developmental Sequence in Small Groups." The idea is that every team must move through these phases to reach the performing pinnacle. High-performing teams deliver extraordinary results again and again, if they're allowed the space to improve their process and grow as a unit. Rimarketing builds that space into the way work is done, giving each team a shot at reaching the high-performance peak. As with individual improvement, however, achieving those heights demands diligence and effort.

Finally, we come to leadership's role in ongoing improvement. In Rimarketing, leaders of all kinds look for ways to become more effective stewards of agility, growing more self-aware and guiding individuals and teams on their own journeys. Being a marketing leader in a traditional environment presents challenges, as evidenced by the short tenure of most CMOs. Rimarketing leadership is more rewarding and less painful, but that's not to say it's effortless. Agile leaders (which is what Rimarketing requires) must know their own weaknesses and strengths so they can address the former and play to the latter.

You'll find more details in the next part of the book, along with concrete steps that Agile leaders can take. For now, take away that getting placed in a leadership role inside a Rimarketing team is not an acknowledgement of perfection achieved. It's the beginning of a lengthy journey of self-discovery and improvement in the service of the teams and the entire marketing organization.

Rimarketing is not analogous to a crash diet that you stick to for a few weeks or months and then abandon as soon as you hit your goal weight. It's a profound lifestyle change that you adopt for as long as you want to enjoy its benefits.

Principle 4: Adaptability

The ability to respond to meaningful change is one of the most valuable parts of any successful Agile system. Adaptability can, of course, get teams into trouble—particularly marketing teams, who navigate lots of outside commitments. If abused, adaptability can become an excuse to overpivot. Beware the leader or stakeholder who says, "I know you've already planned your work for the next few weeks, but you're Agile now. You adapt quickly! Right?" In this principle more than any other, nuance is key.

If you've encountered the original Agile Manifesto for Software Development, you'll recall that one of its core values is "Responding to change over following a plan." These values were written in this format intentionally to signal that given the choice between responding to new information and following a pre-established plan, there is typically more merit in the former. It's not to say that planning goes away, or that we ignore our plans anytime anybody asks us to change for any reason. Later in the manifesto, when outlining the twelve Agile principles, the authors elaborate: "We welcome and plan for change. Agile processes harness change for the customer's competitive advantage."

This is crucial (and quite difficult to achieve). Agile, broadly, and Rimarketing, specifically, recognize that in complex knowledge work like marketing, we can't know everything up front. Our plans will be incomplete and inaccurate. Spending months crafting a perfect plan doesn't make work more likely to succeed; it just delays its start. Instead, we create a series of short-term plans. Opportunities to inspect results and adapt accordingly are built into the process. We'll dig into what this means for Rimarketing in Part Three. For now, take away that adaptation is not the same as interruption.

We want to be able to welcome, plan for, and incorporate change into what we do—when doing so provides a clear, competitive advantage *for our customers*. Remember, in Rimarketing our customers might be internal, and sometimes a rapid change delivers a competitive advantage to an account executive. Rimarketing teams execute that change when the time is right.

We do not, however, respond to every interruption that comes our way. When no plan is safe for even a few days, teams rightly recognize the act of planning as wasteful, and they avoid it. They then end up with ad hoc marketing, chasing shiny objects with no larger objective in mind. As you can imagine, this approach delivers poor outcomes and contributes to burnout among marketing team members (and that depressingly low CMO tenure we discussed earlier).

So adaptability needs to be balanced with stability. The final aspect of this Rimarketing principle to consider is the point at which adaptation flips from being helpful to being frustrating and fatiguing (take a look at Figure 8).

The two circles in the center of the chart—the weekly and quarterly levels—are where adaptability is powerful. Here we learn about the efficacy (or lack thereof) of our day-to-day work, and we adjust our short-term plans in response. These are meaningful changes rather than shiny-object-centered interruptions.

Where we *don't* want to introduce a ton of change is at the annual (or six-month) level, where marketing leadership sets the strategic direction for the department over the long term—based, we hope, on the even larger organizational objectives for that same period. Teams get frustrated when these high-level goals are not set, are set in secret, or are changed over the period they're supposed to cover.

FIGURE 8

Planning Levels

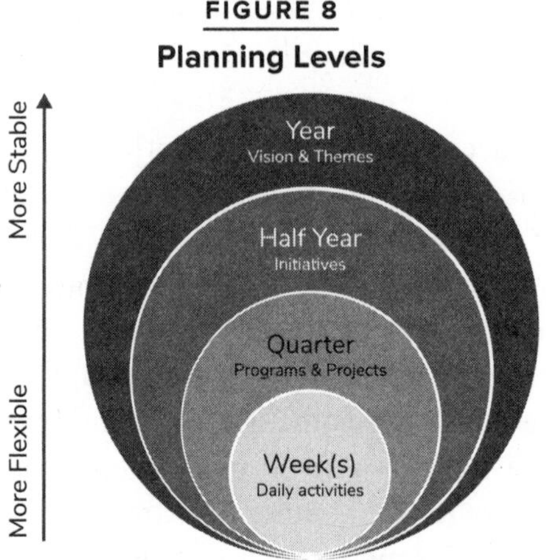

Rimarketing Framework® AgileSherpas.

Each small plan that a team creates uses these big objectives as its guide; changing the objectives is like changing the rules in the middle of a game.

Think of yearly objectives as the destination of a department-wide road trip. The teams are told, "We're starting in San Francisco, and by the end of this year we want to have reached New York City. Along the way we want to see Salt Lake City, Denver, and Boston." The teams come up with a general plan for meeting those targets. They'll probably plan to hit one city per quarter. As the trip begins, they respond to incoming data about road conditions, weather, and wrecks. Each leg of the journey includes small adaptations based on what's really happening. Teams can't plan things perfectly; they can't say, "Drive west in a straight line at fifty-seven miles per hour for exactly 157 minutes, and then change lanes to avoid a slow-moving truck." Drivers constantly adjust their behavior in response to what's going on around them. Adaptability at the micro level is vital for a successful trip.

If, however, they're halfway to a destination and leadership tells them, "Just kidding! We want to go to Denver via Santa Fe," they can't merely adapt their daily plans; they also have to recalibrate their midlevel plan, all while still moving forward toward their goals. This situation is what leads to the common feelings of "building an airplane that's already flying" or "changing the tires on a moving bus."

The same thing happens when the destination simply isn't set. The team can't design effective routes if they don't know where they're heading. Again, they can't do *nothing*, so they thrash about and create a bunch of stuff, but nobody feels satisfied or confident that they're really moving the needle.

In the Rimarketing framework, we welcome and plan for change. We adapt to new information to deliver a competitive advantage to our customers. We don't steer blind, and we don't constantly reroute. Daily and weekly adaptability must dance with stability at the level of yearly objectives.

Principle 5: Trust

At first blush, trust and marketing may seem unrelated. This is largely because marketers and their advertising precursors haven't been reliable stewards of customers' trust. In my previous book, *Death of a Marketer*, I charted the decline of this trust relationship in detail, so I'll summarize it here.

Advertisers and marketers have been barging into living rooms and airwaves and browser windows for decades, which helped establish a trust deficit in the first place. From the moment it became possible to crank out a handbill, entrepreneurs plastered poles and fences with ads. When more portable media like newspapers and magazines came along, fledgling ad agencies weren't far behind, eager to establish a symbiosis that would link ads with the printed word. Then came radio, and, in the United States at least, advertisers appeared on the scene instantly, helpfully offering sponsorships as a means of bringing education, edification, and entertainment into every living room.

When television flickered to life, advertisers could hardly believe their good luck. An invention had arrived that would deliver their messages in irresistible packages that completely grabbed the audience's attention. This powerful new medium had the potential to change everything: how brands defined themselves, how advertisers ran their businesses, and how consumers engaged with content. Already positioned as the benefactors of radio audiences, advertisers knew how to bring TV viewers the programming they craved, complete with ads interspersed among the laughs and learning.

It all sounds sweet and symbiotic in the abstract, but in every case—printed handbills, newspapers, magazines, radio, television, and digital media—we advertisers and marketers eventually wore out our welcome. In our (mostly) legitimate attempts to drive sales for our clients and employers, we abandoned concern for the audience. It's a cycle that has continued for nearly 150 years, and one that has proven itself as magnetic as a black hole.

Rimarketing seeks to counteract this trend by establishing more consistent lines of communication between marketers and audiences. Teams using these processes release marketing work frequently, and they release things when they say they will. When Rimarketing is done well, teams set and keep their publication promises—their publicly stated cadence for releasing certain kinds of work. Many traditional teams don't clearly state their release goals, hoping that by keeping things private their audiences won't notice when they fall behind.

Agile teams are customer-centric (recall Rimarketing Principle 1), which means that a steady drumbeat of content creation isn't enough. We also need to deliver value to audiences, customers, and stakeholders. Marketing to serve, not sell, is the only viable way to approach our profession in the twenty-first century. And we can't serve anyone if we're racing from one missed deadline to the next.

In keeping with the second principle, Radical Transparency, Rimarketing teams share their plans far and wide. They understand that transparency builds trust. Recall the earlier example of Buffer; they share their editorial calendar publicly, so their audience knows what kinds of resources the Buffer content team is planning to deliver and when. Trust can seem like a complicated concept, but it really boils down to this: you state that you'll do something, and then you do it.

Of course, cadence isn't the only meaningful metric in marketing work; delivering terrible stuff frequently is just as bad as doing nothing at all. Emails with missing or broken links and landing pages whose buttons do nothing are just as harmful as a missed deadline. As with most marketing activities, there's a fine line to walk here. Do you delay release of a blog post so a dozen people can spend two weeks reviewing it? Or do you release it on time and risk a missing image or a broken link? When an astute subscriber points out a typo in your weekly newsletter (as happened to me quite recently), do you drop everything and issue a full apology? (I didn't.) Sometimes the error requires attention; at other times it's a form of waste to (as one of my coaching clients would say) keep "polishing the apple" long after it's sufficiently shiny.

Garrett Moon, CEO and cofounder of CoSchedule, tells his marketing team not to go back and fix errors in their old blog posts.[7] I'm an English major and a total word nerd, so for those of you having tiny heart attacks right now, I was right there with you. But here's the thing: if you're fixing typos, you're *not* doing something else more impactful. For Garrett, it's about "prioritizing the work you do to reach your marketing goals ten times faster. Don't do the trivial minutiae that suck productivity away and fail to drive growth."

CoSchedule runs a lean, Agile marketing shop that focuses on doing the right work at the right time. They have results to back up their methods, enjoying 434 percent more page views, 1,222 percent more email subscribers, and 9,360 percent more marketing qualified leads than when they started. Ignoring typos for the win—who knew?[8]

Maybe you're a marketer for a financial services firm, and compliance breathes down your neck every time you log in to Twitter. This exact approach might not work for you. But shipping work regularly, even when it's not absolutely perfect, is a value that can, sometimes paradoxically, help us build trust. After all, we're human. And humans occasionally create typos.

The consumer trust situation is admittedly bad, but it's only one component of trust that marketers need to rebuild for new processes

---

7. Garrett Moon, "Why We Don't Correct Typos," LinkedIn.com, March 6, 2018, www.linkedin.com/pulse/why-we-dont-correct-typos-garrett-moon/.

8. Nathan Ellering, "How to Create a Marketing Strategy that Will Skyrocket Your Results by 9,360 Percent," CoSchedule.com, https://coschedule.com/marketing-strategy/.

to take hold. In addition to reestablishing trust with their customers and audiences, Rimarketing teams are also concerned with:

- trust between leadership and marketing teams
- trust among team members
- trust between stakeholders and marketing teams

Trust between Leadership and Marketing Teams

Rimarketing teams and their leaders complement one another nicely; they're the yin and yang of awesome marketing work. Leaders set strategic goals and clearly communicate them to the marketing teams. Teams ensure that their day-to-day work supports the strategy. The two work in alignment, thanks to the trust built up between them.

When you lose the trust between your marketing teams and leaders, rebuilding it takes time, just as it takes time for your audience to regain trust in your brand when you fail to keep your publication promises. Again, simply state what you plan to do, and then follow through. Once marketing leaders determine when they'll set annual and quarterly goals, they must stick to that schedule. They must also embrace the Radical Transparency principle and ensure that all goals and objectives are documented and publicly available.

When high-level objectives are set, they're set. Annual goals remain in place for the year they're intended to cover, and quarterly goals remain in place for the quarter they're intended to cover. If the high-level goals are vague or contain wiggle room—if they're unclear and imprecise—teams can't trust them. They'll hesitate to commit to short-term plans because they expect the destination to change, forcing them to scramble to react. Take another look at Figure 8, "Planning Levels," and consider again the strategic planning circles. The vision, themes, and epics must be stable so that the stories and tasks can flex. For teams to be able to respond to meaningful change, they must trust that the big picture will hold steady.

Of course, trust is a two-way street. Teams must earn and maintain their leaders' trust by stating their own plans and following through. The team queue, which we'll meet later, solves the first half of that equation. It publicly documents the team's plans so that leaders know exactly what's coming up. If something goes awry and it becomes clear that the stated plan won't come to fruition, the team can maintain trust by exercising their own radical transparency and being open about what's happening.

We *don't* want teams to hide negative information for fear of punitive action by their leaders. As we'll see later, many of the components of Rimarketing support communication between teams and leaders, facilitating trust. Trust rarely appears overnight, but a commitment by both groups to sharing plans, coupled with follow-through, fosters a space in which trust can quickly grow.

Trust among Team Members

We've all worked with people who, for one reason or another, consistently struggle to get their work done well and on schedule. They're classic overpromisers, folks who consistently and dramatically overestimate their ability to get things done. This behavior can decimate a team's trust, particularly when teams are smaller. If everyone needs to pitch in on practically every project, and someone's piece is always missing—always "just about done"—it's a major problem.

In an Agile marketing environment, daily standup meetings reveal these kinds of problems and help illuminate solutions. If someone's daily standup contributions start to sound like a broken record, the team can intervene. Again, we build internal team trust by stating our intentions (without overcommitting) and following through. Practices like daily standup and work visualization automate these steps while revealing trust issues within a team.

We also need for team members to be comfortable talking to their teammates about challenges. They need to trust the team to rally around them and help solve the problem rather than judge them (either openly or silently) for failing to do what they thought they would. This creates what's known as psychological safety.

The People Analytics team at Google is tasked with making life at Google "a little bit better and a lot more productive," and to that end they undertook a massive study of how teams inside Google functioned. Led by Laszlo Bock, People Operations scoured the literature, interviewed Google employees, and diagrammed the complicated relationships between teams. When presenting their findings, Bock reflected, "There's a myth we all carry inside our head. We think we need superstars. But that's not what our research found. You can take a team of average performers, and if you teach them to interact the right way, they'll do things no superstar could ever accomplish."[9]

The "right way," Bock and his team found, could be summarized in five norms:

1. Teams need to believe that their work is important.
2. Teams need to feel that their work is personally meaningful.
3. Teams need clear goals and defined roles.
4. Team members need to know that they can depend on one another.
5. Most important, teams need psychological safety.

All these norms are necessary for Rimarketing teams to create the optimum environment for true agility, but psychological safety is paramount. In the *Journal of Applied Behavioral Science*, Amy Edmondson defined psychological safety as a "shared belief, held by members of a team, that the group is a safe place for taking risks." It is "a sense of confidence that the team will not embarrass, reject, or punish someone for speaking up. . . . It describes a team climate characterized by interpersonal trust and mutual respect in which people are comfortable being themselves."[10]

Attempts at continuous improvement quickly break down when teams feel unsafe sharing potentially contradictory ideas. Process can't improve if no one is willing to open up about the pieces that need adjustment. Psychological safety not only increases a team's morale and productivity; it's a prerequisite for agility.

But how do we cultivate it?

Team leaders foster psychological safety by modeling these behaviors in their own interactions with the team—even, and especially, when it would be easy to avoid doing so. In reviewing his exhaustive research on the topic, Charles Duhigg puts it this way:

---

9. Charles Duhigg, *Smarter Faster Better: The Transformative Power of Real Productivity* (New York: Random House), 81–82.

10. Amy Edmondson, "Psychological Safety and Learning in Work Teams," *Administrative Science Quarterly*, June, 1999), pp. 350–383.

> There are always good reasons for choosing behaviors that undermine psychological safety. It is often more efficient to cut off debate, to make a quick decision, to listen to whoever knows the most and ask others to hold their tongues. But a team will become an amplification of its internal culture, for better or worse. Study after study shows that while psychological safety might be less efficient in the short run, it's more productive over time.[11]

Team members themselves foster psychological safety by sharing control of the team with teammates. We demonstrate that we're actually listening by repeating what someone just said and responding respectfully. If a teammate seems upset, we react with compassion instead of pretending nothing is amiss. By ceding control to the group and consistently displaying our empathy, we create a stronger, more Agile team environment.

As you can imagine, we're more likely to achieve psychological safety, and other conditions for high performance, when a team stays together. We'll come back to this issue later, but for now keep in mind that the more a team is persistent, the more likely teammates are to learn to trust one another.

In a high-performing Rimarketing team, individual members must trust each other to contribute effectively (and on time). This internal trust helps to build up the other kinds, including trust with audiences and with internal stakeholders.

Trust between Stakeholders and Marketing Teams

If a trust gap exists between marketers and their audiences, a trust chasm divides marketers from their internal stakeholders. Every time we commit to providing sales-enablement collateral and then miss the deadline, the chasm widens. Every time the CTO expects us to buy a new piece of martech this quarter and we can't get our act together soon enough to make a decision, the chasm widens. Thanks to this recurring cycle, many marketing teams I've coached have been referred to as "black holes"—places where work requests go in but nothing ever comes out.

11. Duhigg, *Smarter Faster Better*, 85.

Part of the blame for this perception can be laid at the feet of an organization's processes, but marketing teams are also victims of their own accommodating natures and marketing's position at the hub of brand experience. Because marketing is a vital part of how customers interact with a company's products and services, most people inside an organization need things from the marketing department. Believing that their needs are crucial and time sensitive, these people make demands of marketers (with varying degrees of civility and detail). Marketers want to be obliging, useful colleagues, so they agree to all requests and then run around like headless chickens trying, and of course failing, to get it all done.

Unfortunately, experiment after experiment proves that the more we work on, the longer everything takes. Multitasking has been shown to reduce productivity by 40 percent, according to a study in the *Journal of Experimental Psychology*.[12] This is not a pleasant equation, but we've all felt its effects when staring down a monster to-do list. What's more, without a formal work-management process in place to limit our work in progress, we say yes to every incoming request, and then everything takes forever.

This painfully common scenario is no doubt the source of some 2016 data from Workfront's State of Marketing Report, which found that 98 percent of marketers experience conflict with other departments.[13] Ouch.

To bridge the chasm between marketing and our internal stakeholders, we must—wait for it—state our intentions and follow through on them. This often involves a serious winnowing of the things we're already doing. In other words, we have to get better at saying no. MarketingProfs' 2019 Marketer Happiness Report discovered that 41 percent of marketers say no only a few times per year to projects that aren't

12. American Psychological Association, "Multitasking: Switching Costs," March 20, 2006, https://www.apa.org/research/action/multitask.

13. "The US State of Marketing Work Report, 2016–2017," https://www.workfront.com/sites/default/files/resource/file_pdf/2018-05/2016-17-u-s-state-of-marketing-work-report.pdf.

aligned with their goals, and another 26 percent reported they don't have the authority to *ever* say no.[14]

We'll tackle this problem toward the end of the book. For now, we need to acknowledge that behavior by both parties—marketers and their stakeholders—has historically contributed to dysfunctional dynamics. Paradoxically, only by empowering marketers to say no and to focus on high-value activities can we deliver on other groups' expectations and begin to cross the yawning trust gap.

Principle 6: Bias toward Action

Objects at rest tend to stay at rest. Objects in motion tend to stay in motion. Our good friend inertia may have initially been theorized to explain the behavior of the physical world, but it applies to knowledge work as well. The hardest part about exerting almost any kind of effort is getting started. But if we can get in the habit of getting started, if our default mode is to act, to be in motion, then we begin to have a bias toward action.

To be clear, I don't advocate action for action's sake. We don't want to do something just so that we can be doing something. Our preference in Rimarketing is to take informed action based on the powerful combination of our marketing expertise and relevant data. But when we're faced with the choice between doing something and doing nothing while we wait for more data, we tend to act. Acting based on directional data is better than standing still and waiting for the overwhelming evidence that supports our theory.

However, when we act on incomplete information, we need to realize that we are doing so. Such action must be undertaken in the spirit of experimentation, meaning that we have a clearly articulated hypothesis, defined data points, and established measurement capabilities all set up before we begin.

---

14. "2019 Marketer Happiness Report," January 31, 2019, https://www.marketingprofs.com/content/report/39801/2019-marketer-happiness-report.

The Pareto Principle and GEFN

This Rimarketing principle is one of many ways that we strive to live by the Pareto Principle, the notion that 80 percent of marketing's value comes from 20 percent of the work. Our goal is to figure out what that 20 percent is and get it done quickly. Most of the time it's impossible to accurately predict which 20 percent that will be. Since we can discover it only through releasing, inspecting, and adapting our work, the sooner we get going, the sooner we start learning, and the sooner that all-powerful 20 percent emerges.

Closely related to the Pareto Principle is GEFN, which stands for "good enough for now." Love this slogan. Embrace it. Get it tattooed on your forehead if you have to. Marketers need to get comfortable with GEFN. Yes, we could spend another six weeks polishing up a campaign until it's award-worthy. But is the return on that investment of time worth it? Would we rather have it out in the world, as is, teaching us through its performance and delivering results for those six weeks? Is it, in fact, good enough for now?

Here is one of many great things about marketing having gone almost entirely digital: electronic promotions are far easier to change than physical ones. When we put out a GEFN campaign that starts taking off, we know right away that it's a winner because of our data-collection plan. We can immediately improve it (if necessary). If our GEFN campaign looks like a dud, digital capabilities mean we can jump in and iterate. These interventions wouldn't have been possible before social media and the internet, but all these digital channels are responsible for our insanely complex profession. We might as well put them to work for us.

One final note about GEFN and the bias toward action: GEFN differs from organization to organization. If you're in a greatly regulated environment like financial services or pharmaceuticals, your "good enough" level is higher than that of a software company operating with scant legal oversight.

But whether you wait for regulatory review or fly unencumbered through your marketing plan, you'll shorten the path to success when you adopt a bias toward action.

Principle 7: Courage

I close with this principle because it's only fair to acknowledge that what I'm asking you to do—radically alter the way you work—isn't easy. As you might suspect, having made it this far through the list of principles, successfully implementing Rimarketing requires serious change and difficult choices. Both of these, in turn, demand courage.

As the saying goes, courage doesn't mean not being afraid; it means acting in spite of your fear. This principle, likewise, doesn't mean you never experience worry, doubt, skepticism, or anxiety about what you're up to. It means you proceed anyway. And, as with the bias toward action, courage doesn't mean barreling blindly ahead and ignoring all warning signs. Courage can be well informed and data driven; having the information to back up your courage doesn't make it any less admirable.

So what does courage look like in a Rimarketing organization? It comes with two distinguishing characteristics: conviction and considered action.

Conviction is confidence that you're on the right track. It drives your need to do something or say something. From my days growing up in the Southern Baptist church, I remember fire-and-brimstone preachers talking about the Holy Spirit "convicting" members of the congregation. Don't get me wrong—I'm not implying that Rimarketing should guide you with religious fervor. But the sense of that statement rings true for me. Some unseen force that you believe in, whether it's guiding principles for doing amazing professional work or a spirit nudging you to be a better person, prompts you to act.

Conviction brings with it a need for considered action—as contrasted with impulsive or brash *reaction*. In a Rimarketing department, considered action might mean pointing out, as tactfully as possible, that the new campaign is all about us and not so much about the customer. It might mean taking a teammate aside to quietly discuss clinging to the status quo versus embracing a bias toward action.

You also want to consider the actions that could most effectively remedy the problem. Privately pointing out a misguided focus may reveal to someone a gap they were unaware of. Then they can adjust accordingly, and the team won't waste effort creating a campaign that's destined to underperform.

Of course, that's an ideal scenario; courageous actions don't always play out so beautifully. But even if your considered action backfires, it's always preferable to a spontaneous, impetuous reaction to your convictions.

Also remember the need to establish trust and psychological safety within a team. Ill-considered outbursts erode relationships and endanger the team's ability to effectively execute other aspects of the Rimarketing framework. You may feel strongly convicted to point out a flaw or make a comment, and sometimes doing so in the moment is the most beneficial course of action. Pause a beat before you speak, however, and give yourself time to consider whether your courage-driven action will build or erode trust. As with all the Rimarketing principles, we need to strive for balance.

Antipatterns to Avoid

The bulk of Part One has covered the positive side of the principles: what they mean, how to know you're putting them into practice—all that nice stuff. Before we move on, we need to address a few common antipatterns: scenarios that indicate movement in the *wrong* direction. Think of these as check-engine lights, alerting you to the immediate need for system maintenance. If you see any of them happening, it means you're veering away from core Rimarketing principles.

Antipattern #1: Rewarding Empire Building

The marketing department of a major enterprise spent two years building a massively successful Agile marketing practice. They released faster, their team members were more satisfied, and they enjoyed better ROI on all their efforts. Enter the new senior marketing leader with no interest in Agile values. He followed his established playbook, building his own pet teams to work on his pet projects. He pulled people off the high-performing cross-functional teams that had been built, painstakingly, on the backs of many experiments.

Team members, one after another, were affected by this empire building. Each questioned the wisdom of staying on the existing Agile teams, which were no longer being supported. The obvious career move was to join a specialized team championed by the new leader. Other marketing leaders, sensing a change in the winds, reverted to their old patterns of behavior. Traditional command-and-control management styles returned, with leaders grabbing for power (and high performers) to achieve their own objectives. The Agile teams died.

Executive leadership could have stopped this behavior instantly. (See Principle 7, Courage, above.) Instead, the pedigreed new hire was fully indulged and was, in fact, rewarded, leaving his Agile marketing peers little alternative except to following his example.

This is the epitome of Antipattern #1. For Rimarketing in particular (and Agile marketing in general) to succeed, marketing leaders must change their behavior. If the organization continues to reward non-Agile behavior, leaders have every reason to avoid change.

Rewards may come in the form of public praise, promotions, or raises, or they may be more implicit and private. Either way, everyone at every level feels rewarded in one way or another. It's always clear what behavior is valued at the highest levels, and individual contributors emulate those behaviors.

Encouraging empire building—or any other actions that circumvent the team-centric focus of Rimarketing and Agile—undermines trust, destroys high-performing teams, and sets even the most advanced marketing processes back months or years. Don't let your new hire, no matter how great the pedigree, circumvent your process.

Antipattern #2: Tolerating Underperforming Individuals

If empire-building execs live at one end of the dysfunction spectrum, the other end is home to underperforming team members. Turning a blind eye as marketing leaders skirt principles and break processes destroys psychological safety. Pretending that everyone on the team is pulling his or her weight when it's not true is an equally destructive antipattern.

Rimarketing processes, as we'll soon see, create visibility into all kinds of performance. Knowing what's going on is the only way to improve it, and sometimes what's going on isn't great. If the process improvements uncover serious personnel problems, they can't be ignored. People make up the process, and you can't build an outstanding process on substandard performers.

Some marketers spend their careers hiding behind busyness; they're good at moving, but less good at delivering results. Others are territorial, preferring to tend to their little corner rather than ensuring larger team success. Still others lack necessary job skills and have become adept at concealing that fact.

Whatever the manifestation, you can't tolerate underperformers. We'll touch on this a bit more in Part Two, "People." For now, know that pretending that everyone is great when they clearly aren't sends you down the wrong path. Empowered, autonomous teams uncover these problems quickly; ignoring the difficulties sends the message that competence and high performance aren't *really* that important. That's a recipe for underperformance across the board.

Antipattern #3: Inability to Track and Measure Marketing's True Impact

A value at the core of Agile marketing is a preference for validated learning over opinions and conventions. This just makes sense to many of us, especially in the era of big data, artificial intelligence, and machine learning. If we can rely on proven information instead of unsubstantiated intuition, we do so. This antipattern emerges when we simply lack access to the data that validate our learning.

If you can't accurately measure, track, or attribute marketing work, you can't rely on data-backed insight. Decision making then comes down to who has the better title or can shout the loudest.

Does this mean that you can't be Agile or implement Rimarketing if you lack end-to-end, bulletproof data and analytics capabilities? No. But if you don't have *any* insight into the quantitative side of marketing, you're going to struggle. Without any validated learning, opinions and conventions win the day. It can be challenging to run even a simple A/B test, because whoever's idea isn't supported by the outcome can simply blame poor data quality and demand that their idea be tried anyway.

Antipattern #4: Weak Understanding of Customers and an Inability or Unwillingness to Learn

A similar gap emerges when marketing is up against a lack of connection to the people they're communicating with. When an organization has a weak relationship with customers, marketing's job (and its ability to behave based on Agile principles) becomes more difficult.

Agile in general, and Rimarketing in particular, places the customer at the center. We build teams around stages of the customer journey rather than around functional capabilities. We document our work via customer stories rather than twenty-page creative briefs. Every facet of the system is set up to bring us closer to our customers.

If you start a hundred miles from your customers, that connection strengthens slowly, and if the gap seems so wide that you never start to bridge it, nothing changes. Problems crop up when ignorance about the customer meets an unwillingness to learn.

When you lack customer knowledge, commit to putting time, energy, and money toward getting to know them. Learning (preferably the validated kind) has to be a huge part of marketing's job. This might mean that you appear to slow down for a while; maybe you publish less often, write fewer emails, and dial back your event sponsorships—whatever it takes. Be willing to do the legwork required to reconnect with customers.

Some marketing groups struggle to know their customers. They're aware of the lack of connection, but the unrelenting demand to hit targets drives them to just keep going. There's no time to learn, no time for conversations with customers. The lethal combination of ignorance and an inability or unwillingness to remedy it makes up this fourth antipattern.

Antipattern #5: Bias toward the Status Quo

This antipattern is the evil twin of the sixth Rimarketing principle, Bias toward Action. In this scenario, "change" is a dirty word. Teams and their members have a death grip on the status quo. Highly traditional industries are most prone to this failing, but it can happen anywhere.

You know you're on this path when you hear things like "That would never work *here*," or "Sure, but our problems are way more complex," or any other variation on "We're snowflakes whose unique work is immune to all forms of process improvement." What's really being said is, "Change is scary and we don't like it."

In this antipattern you might also see individuals who are closely identified with their work. Long-time employees, in particular, often come to equate their professional identify with the way work gets done. When leaders say things like, "We're going to overhaul our process to be more effective and efficient," these people hear, "You're bad at your job and have failed to get things done the way I want."

Whether or not it comes from a place of inertia and fear, a bias toward "the way we've always done things" is one of the most insidious antipatterns you can encounter.

Antipattern #6: Inability to Say No

This antipattern may *sound* less formidable than the others, but it can derail Rimarketing adoption and undermine an Agile mindset in a heartbeat. I underestimated this antipattern until I saw data from the MarketingProfs 2019 Marketer Happiness Report, reproduced in Figure 9.

I mean come on, my fellow marketers! More than half of us never, or virtually never, say no! Another quarter of us completely lack the authority to say no. Ever! *Even when the request clearly doesn't fit with our priorities.*

You can't improve your process at any level if no one in your marketing department can say no. Everyone—and I mean everyone—must be capable and comfortable uttering a negative answer when asked to undertake new work. The only way to do the right work at the right time is to eliminate the wrong work, and that means saying no.

Easily my favorite line from the Agile Manifesto is "Simplicity, maximizing the amount of work not done, is essential." You can't follow this wisdom if you say yes to every request that comes your way. We'll dive into the fun data behind all of this in Part Four, "Prac-

FIGURE 9

Can Marketers say "No" to Projects that Don't Fit Their Goals/Priorities?

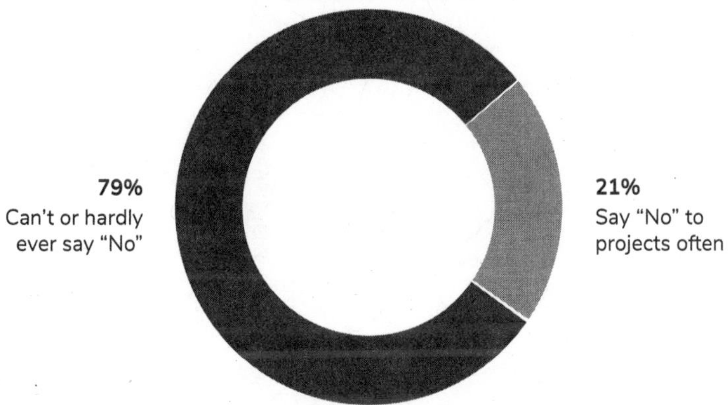

Source: MarketingProfs 2019 Marketer Happiness Report.

tices," but for now take heed: if you have people in your marketing department who can't say no, address that antipattern ASAP.

Dealing with Antipatterns

When you encounter an antipattern, don't despair. Change often comes with a dip in output and productivity as individuals and teams internalize the shift. The Swiss psychiatrist Elisabeth Kübler-Ross developed a model for predicting this pattern (see Figure 10).

As the figure shows, we don't immediately enjoy massive gains from any kind of change. There's inevitably a period of adjustment. People first enter denial, hoping that the change can somehow be avoided. You may even see an uptick in productivity as people strive to avoid the difficult process of change by working harder. Then, when the change happens anyway, a period of frustration and depression occurs. To move past this phase we begin to experiment, to try new ways of integrating the change into established processes. Once we do that, it's possible to embrace the change as positive and enjoy the benefits of doing things more effectively.

Every team will go through this process in response to change, as will every member of the team. Some people race through it quickly

FIGURE 10

Kübler-Ross Change Curve

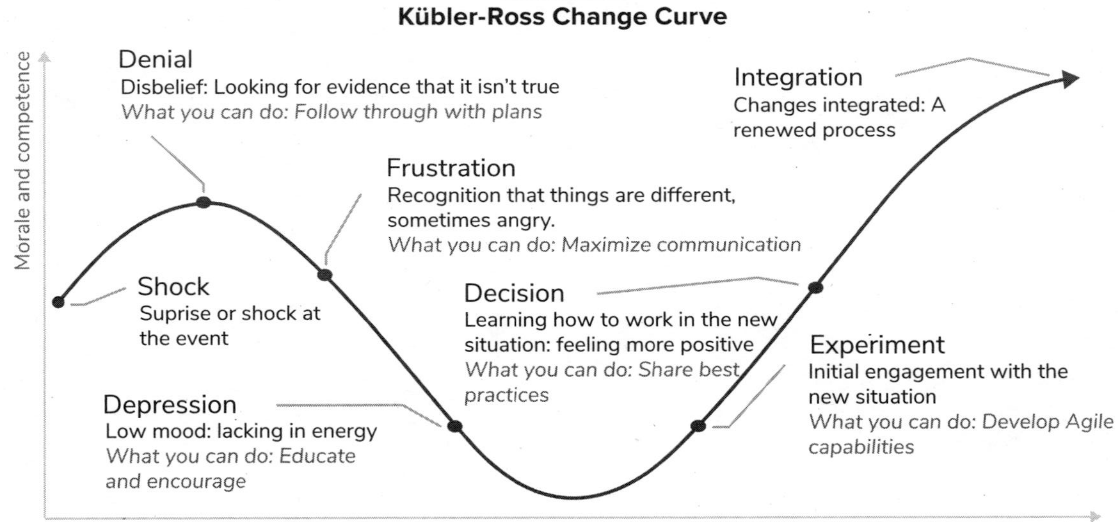
Morale and competence
Denial
Disbelief: Looking for evidence that it isn't true
What you can do: Follow through with plans
Shock
Suprise or shock at the event
Frustration
Recognition that things are different, sometimes angry.
What you can do: Maximize communication
Depression
Low mood: lacking in energy
What you can do: Educate and encourage
Decision
Learning how to work in the new situation: feeling more positive
What you can do: Share best practices
Experiment
Initial engagement with the new situation
What you can do: Develop Agile capabilities
Integration
Changes integrated: A renewed process
Time

Source: Author.

and excitedly, while others get mired in the pit of depression. Allow team members to experience their initial negative responses, and be prepared to help them experiment with the new ways of working and internalize the change at their own pace. Ideally, have someone available to help coach team members through the early, tempestuous stages of adoption. Trainers and consultants who have seen major change happen can provide good perspective, and they can help guide people along their journey to acceptance and, eventually, awesomeness.

PART 2

PEOPLE
The Peskiest (and Most Powerful) Part of Agile Systems

> Beyond the company results the team is asked to produce, teams need something to strive for—something to change the hamster wheel into a journey of their own making.
>
> LYSSA ADKINS, *COACHING AGILE TEAMS*

EVERY SYSTEM OF KNOWLEDGE-WORKERS is made up of the same highly complex, convoluted, and confusing components: people. Humans, unpredictable and weird creatures that we are, make organizational design far more difficult than it could be. Because it's designed for use on the planet Earth, Rimarketing must consider the idiosyncrasies of people. This part of the book describes the different roles that make up a high-functioning Rimarketing system, from individuals to teams to leaders.

We'll first meet the execution team, the building block of every unit within a Rimarketing system. Execution teams, as their name implies, focus on execution, so they rely on others, namely the strategy group, to help direct their efforts. In larger organizations we find another group, known simply as the leadership team, that connects marketing's work to larger strategic goals. In big organizations where multiple execution teams, and sometimes multiple strategy groups, need to collaborate, we may also encounter a team of teams. This hefty collection is known as a pack. As summarized in Table 1, each of these cohorts has unique responsibilities that can't be fulfilled by anyone else.

TABLE 1

Groups and Their Responsibilities

Group	Role
Execution team	Owners of the "how." Turn strategic priorities into reality. Focused on doing amazing work as a high-performing unit.
Strategy group	Owners of the "what" for one or more execution teams. Set clear direction for execution teams to follow. Provide direction when needed but does not dictate execution.
Leadership team	Found primarily in larger organizations. Set long-term strategy at a departmental level. Interface with other departments and strategy groups.
Pack	A collection of execution teams and strategy groups that share a meaningful reason to collaborate. Only found in enterprise marketing organizations.

Individuals and teams are quite powerful in their own right; you won't find any glorification of higher-ups as the repository of sacred strategy. Instead, imagine a Rimarketing organization as a garden. Its ability to bear fruit depends on all its components working in harmony.

The Unstoppable Force of High-Performing Teams

Many teams I've coached have bemoaned the presence of low performers and their detrimental effect on agility. Whether they're perceived as unskilled, uninterested, or just plain lazy, these people can seriously drag down a team. The obvious solution would seem to be hiring a whole bunch of smart, experienced, motivated people and putting them together. Sadly, efforts at doing just that have repeatedly failed in all kinds of organizations. A long list of companies have burned through cash bringing on stars, only to find their fancy new hires shunned by colleagues who resent their preferential treatment.

Unable to connect to teammates or access any organizational knowledge, the supposed superstar never shines very bright.

Instead of fixating on finding star individuals, we need to create the conditions for high-performing teams to thrive. When this happens, people enjoy the magical combination of autonomy, mastery, and purpose that promotes motivation in all kinds of digital knowledge work. The teams accomplish more than their individual members could ever have achieved alone. And the company enjoys better products, more effective marketing, and a stronger bottom line. In short, high-performing teams benefit every individual in an organization. So in Rimarketing, we follow the advice of Agile coach Lyssa Adkins (whose quote opened this chapter) and expect high performance from every team.

With that said, there's no firm definition of high performance in Rimarketing, because each team is striving to achieve different outcomes. Each team also has its own unique dynamics, so high performance will manifest differently across groups. Jon Katzenbach and Douglas Smith's definition of teams that "outperform all reasonable expectations"[1] is a good guidepost and will be as strict as we get in our efforts to pin down high performance for Rimarketing teams. You will, however, always be able to spot true high-performing teams by the work they do—and the relatively short amount of time it takes them to get it done.

We may be unable to fully define high-performing teams, but we can identify key characteristics they share. You'll notice that these align closely with Rimarketing values, and that they are reflected in the processes and practices we'll explore in later parts of the book. High-performing teams are

- self-organizing rather than role- or title-based
- empowered to make decisions
- confident that as a team they can solve any problem
- committed to team success rather than success at any cost

1. Jon R. Katzenbach and Douglas K. Smith, "The Wisdom of Teams: Creating the High-Performance Organization," McKinsey & Company, 1993, http://www.mit.edu/~mbarker/teaming/team04.txt, 91.

- owners of their decisions and commitments
- motivated by trust, not fear or anger
- consensus-driven, able to diverge during ideation and then converge on a shared decision
- in a constant state of constructive disagreement

Execution Teams: Cultivating Performance

Individual contributors are the plants in the garden. Execution teams are the beds into which they are collected so they can be supported as they grow. As their name implies, execution teams are where work gets done inside the Rimarketing system. Execution teams are built on the idea that a single beautiful flower or one high-producing plant isn't enough. One lovely bloom won't entice the swarm of bees needed to pollinate all the surrounding plants; no matter how many fruits one plant produces, it won't feed an entire community. We need groups that can accomplish more than their individual contributors could achieve alone, and that's why we construct execution teams.

But before we fully dive into the structure, composition, and responsibilities of the execution team, we need to see how they fit into the larger Rimarketing structure (see Figure 11).

Depending on the size and complexity of your marketing organization, you may have anywhere from one to one hundred execution teams. The number is less important than the reason that teams come together and how they're evaluated. Rimarketing execution teams require a transcendent purpose that creates a serious need for collaboration. Then, as they work together over time, they need just one or two key performance indicators (KPIs) to evaluate their success (more on all of this shortly).

Individual Contributors: Cross-Functionality in an Agile Environment

It's time now to address the people who actually make up a high-performing team: individual contributors. They have certain expectations put on them within the Rimarketing framework, but their primary focus is to do outstanding work as part of a high-performing team. That *sounds* straightforward, but members of execution teams

FIGURE 11

Execution Teams in Rimarketing

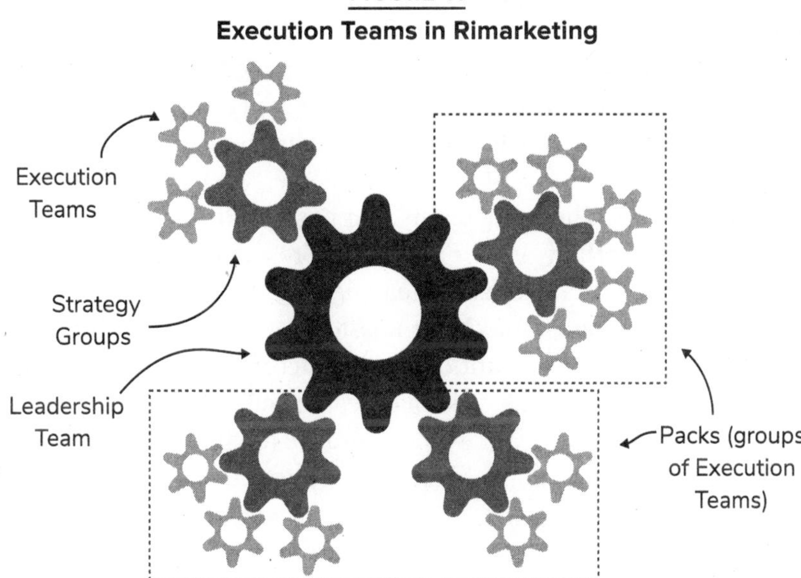

Rimarketing Framework® AgileSherpas.

have certain characteristics that contribute to great success. The first of these is cross-functionality, or the ability to work on a wide variety of tasks. For individuals, this means a broad foundational skill set supplemented by a few core specialties. We can visualize this as a T-shaped marketer, a concept illustrated earlier, in Figure 6 (see page 16):

This simple idea can be quite disruptive to marketing specialists accustomed to focusing on their niche, but it's a shift worth making. By deliberately broadening the type of work that people can contribute to, we can exponentially increase the velocity of their team. If I've previously been focused exclusively on copywriting, I can contribute only a small sliver of the work my team's responsible for. The vertical bar of my T goes deep, but the horizontal bar is short. Through pairing (the practice of actually sitting with someone who has the skill you're trying to develop) and training, I may eventually be able to assist with other work, such as scheduling social media, designing email campaigns, or helping with the designs that accompany my copy.

As you can imagine, this type of development doesn't happen accidentally. It requires slack, or moments of downtime, to enable a widening of the top bar of the T. Teams that need to cultivate additional skill sets should set aside a percentage of their working time to actively build new capabilities within their members.

Just as we have cross-functional people, we can have cross-functional teams. These are teams that possess all the skills necessary to complete the work for which they're responsible. The idea behind cross-functionality at the team level is that it reduces dependence on other groups, making it possible for a team to commit to completing a certain amount of work in a certain amount of time. In traditional Agile teams, this manifests itself as creating a small backlog of work that a team would complete during a sprint. In Rimarketing, we want to establish cross-functional teams that are minimally dependent on others, but the *way* we achieve this evolves.

We'll discuss this concept more later as we begin to explore organizational design and team structure, but for now let's distinguish between the Rimarketing approach and the more traditional Agile way.

Iterative Agile frameworks like Scrum hope that nearly everyone in a team is a cross-functional individual; failing that, they want to have all necessary skills contained within the team. For instance, UX (user experience), front- and back-end development, and quality assurance (QA) might all sit together on a single team. When it's time to create a new Agile team, they copy this structure, bringing together different UX, development, and QA people.

In marketing we rarely have this type of equitable head count, which is why Rimarketing doesn't call for carbon-copy teams. Instead, we begin with our why.

Why does this new team exist?

What objective do we expect them to deliver?

How will they be measured?

Only once we've answered these questions do we determine what level of cross-functionality is required to meet those goals. A team focused on demand-generation activities needs very different skills from a team that's responsible for retention, for instance. In each case the team design will be different. Ultimately, we want a team that's able to autonomously deliver value. The less they depend on other groups, even other teams within the Rimarketing organization, the better.

In addition to being as cross-functional as possible, individual contributors in Rimarketing need to be more entrepreneurial than your average marketer. Remember that a core value of Rimarketing is to be biased toward action. This means that we can't have team members sitting around waiting for someone to tell them what to do. They take a look at organizational priorities, team commitments, and, most important, customer needs, and they find valuable work to do. (The Rimarketing processes and practices described in Parts Three and Four of the book will cover these activities in more detail.) Overall, the system works to create artifacts that facilitate entrepreneurial behavior. Likewise, we encourage a more holistic view of team success rather than a focus on merely executing work that aligns to an individual's subject-matter expertise.

These kinds of group-centric behaviors are particularly important as Rimarketing matures. As quickly as possible, we need to empower teams and push decision-making capabilities as close to the work (and to the customers it serves) as possible. The Rimarketing principle of trust plays a major role here. We need to collect strong, capable team members who can make intelligent decisions about how to add value to customers and audiences.

If they can't make those decisions, leaders need to ask themselves what information is missing. How can individual contributors and execution teams get the knowledge they need to make good choices on a daily basis? If the issue is a lack of trust rather than an absence of information, systemic issues are likely at play. Training, alignment around brand standards, documented process guidelines—all of these may need to be put in place to safely move decision making down to the team and individual contributor level.

As you can imagine, setting up a team that functions at this level isn't an overnight endeavor. It takes months to build a high-performing team, and even longer to scale that success across the wider marketing function. This means that it's crucial to hire carefully into an existing Rimarketing team or system. Depending on where you are in terms of team development, new interviewing and onboarding practices are likely to be necessary. The emerging field of Agile human resources has much to offer us here, so look to this group as strategic partners.

If your Rimarketing department is a garden, think of hiring as planting the right seeds. If you make the wrong call, you'll grow the wrong fruit. Or even worse, you may introduce a weed into your thriving ecosystem.

The Making of an Execution Team

To enable them to perform at their highest level, we structure execution teams according to the following guidelines:

- **Shared purpose:** Ideally teams form around the shared goal of delivering value to customers. Their purpose should be overarching and clear.
- **A few clear KPIs:** One of the most important ways that an execution team achieves high performance is through its ability to say no to incoming requests. Their core KPIs are the filter through which all stakeholder asks must pass; work that won't deliver on an execution team's KPI won't get accepted by the team.
- **Owners of the "how":** The leadership team and strategy groups will be asked to own the "what"—to clearly tell others what objectives are crucial to marketing and organizational success. It's the execution team that gets to own the "how": the ways they choose to achieve those objectives.
- **Cross-functionality:** Teams should contain all the necessary skills to execute the work for which they're responsible. Interdependencies create bottlenecks and delays; avoid them whenever possible.

- **Reasonable size:** Execution teams are small, ideally between four and ten people. There are options for organizing teams outside this size range, but the research is clear: smaller teams get more done.
- **Stable point of contact:** One person, the team lead (whom we'll meet shortly), should act as the buffer between the team and its stakeholders. This role frees up individual contributors to focus on executing outstanding work.
- **Strategic connection:** The team lead also connects the team to a larger strategy, at both the marketing and organizational levels. Together with the shared purpose, this connection provides a clear North Star for the team to work toward.
- **Psychological safety:** Teams need to feel safe speaking their minds, even if that means fundamentally disagreeing with leaders or fellow team members.

One of the most defective parts of traditional marketing organizations is the way we've been setting up teams. A project idea comes along, and we bring together a group of people to work on it. If we're lucky, that project has been vetted for its ability to deliver marketing and business value, but often it's a mandate from sales or executive leaders with little clearly stated value behind it. The project "team" (I use quotation marks here deliberately, because this kind of group doesn't meet my definition of a team, as you'll soon find out) usually doesn't get a say on whether or not they're going to be in the group; they're basically conscripted.

Under the guidance of a project manager, a project kickoff meeting of some kind takes place, lots of up-front planning and scheduling happens, and work theoretically begins. I say "theoretically" because without fail all the people in this new group are already part of other project "teams." That means their days are already full of to-dos, deadlines, and meetings for other projects. And yet now they have an additional commitment.

As we'll discover in Part Four, "Practices," this enormous task list doesn't signal that someone is important or valuable. Instead, it's a clear sign that everything they do is going to take exponentially longer than it should. As team members struggle to juggle dozens of different obligations (each of which is someone's number-one priority that needs attention RIGHT NOW), they're continually behind. They get dragged to meeting after meeting, because somehow we've begun to equate meetings with meaning. The more meetings we have, the more meaningful our work must be. That's simply untrue, and the meeting mania sucks away productive time, leaving tiny pockets here and there during which we can attempt actual work. When that effort fails, we work at home and on the weekends. And yet all our work drags on.

These delays simply don't mesh with our digital world where people expect real-time, personalized marketing messaging, and they're directly correlated to our project-centric "team" design. When people are on multiple teams, they can't limit the amount of work they have in progress. They can't say no to anything, their to-do list grows by the day, and projects take months to reach an audience that's grown accustomed to instant communication. No wonder marketing has become a black hole.

To combat this pernicious arrangement, Rimarketing teams are never organized around projects.

I repeat: in a Rimarketing system you will not be forming project teams.

Instead, we bring teams together around a shared purpose or customer-centric outcome, which can be measured through a tangible KPI or two.

For instance, we might create teams focused on customers at a particular stage of their buying journey. Perhaps we have a team concentrating on generating new leads and creating an addressable audience, another focused on converting those people into paying customers, and a third upselling, cross-selling, and retaining those hard-won customers.

Another option is to design teams that specialize in marketing to a particular persona across their entire buying journey. You could also have teams supporting different product lines or regions. The actual makeup of the teams will depend on what you're marketing and to whom, but the important thing is to move away from project "teams" and create groups that can stay together for the long term, working to serve a particular kind of customer.

In this Rimarketing arrangement, it should be very clear who's on a particular team and who's not. In the old world of project groups, some people are part of the group only because they need to remain informed about the work happening around a project; they're sort of part of the group, but not really. Likewise, some members are involved in the early stages of the group's work, but not so much the completion stages. Sometimes they're unsure if they're still on the team (but they have to go to all the meetings).

By contrast, Rimarketing teams have set members, and everyone knows who they are. This arrangement is crucial, because it allows us to reverse the typical flow of work in a marketing department. Historically, marketing organizations move the people to the work; in Rimarketing, we move the work to the people. This notion bears exploring further because it's a significant departure from how most marketing organizations work.

Traditionally, someone in an organization has an idea for a project. If they're senior enough or if they convince enough people that their idea is a good one, they'll get permission to put together a team. So they grab a group of individuals who have the necessary skills, and those people become the project team. Depending on my skill set and my level of seniority, I could be tapped to join lots of projects. Being so chosen is often seen as a good thing; it means I'm valuable and lots of people want to work with me. But it also means that I have to go to meetings for every single one of those projects, provide status updates to all the project owners, coordinate with team members for each project, and somehow also find time to get actual work done for the project. If I'm very unlucky, I also have a "day job"—recurring activities that aren't related to a particular project but that I somehow still have to finish in the midst of the other demands.

You see the problem here (and perhaps you live it every day): too many demands, not enough time.

In Rimarketing, we turn this arrangement on its head. Instead of pulling together a new team every time we launch a new project, campaign, or initiative, we look at the existing teams and decide which

FIGURE 12

Flowing Work the Right Way

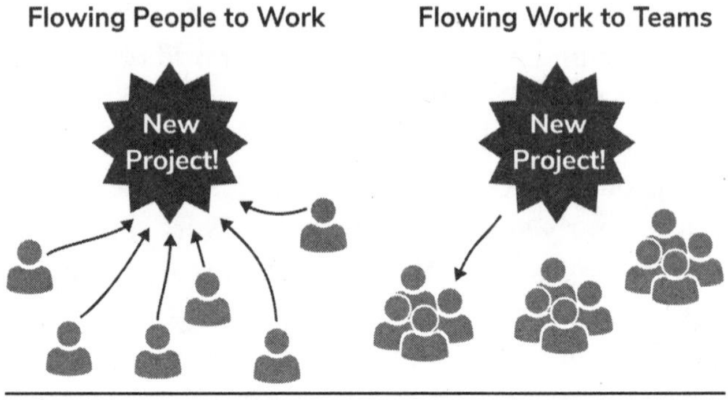

Flowing People to Work | Flowing Work to Teams

New Project! New Project!

Rimarketing Framework® AgileSherpas.

of them is most capable of executing the work, as illustrated in Figure 12.

If, in the image above, one team has about 80 percent of the skills needed to get a new project done, the project will go into their queue and they'll be responsible for completing it. They might still need to collaborate with another team or tap an agency or freelancer to supplement their skill set, but the project will live with them. Their queue then consists of multiple kinds of work, all of which are focused on the audience, stage of the journey, or other customer-centric objectives they own.

Flowing work this way creates stable, persistent, high-performing teams that can collaborate and innovate in amazing ways. It also frees people from the overwork and overwhelm of simultaneously sitting on multiple project "teams."

This isn't simply an altruistic move to make people's lives easier or to create greater employee engagement (although both of those are laudable goals and expected outcomes). Project-based teams are one of the chief causes of excessive context switching in modern marketing arrangements. Although particularly prevalent in marketing, context switching is a serious problem in knowledge work in general. Context switching is the real name for what we often call multitasking. It happens when our brains have to move from one area of focus to another.

Research has revealed that humans aren't capable of actually multitasking; we just jump from task to task. But our brains need time to process the jump. They can't instantly refocus. The time it takes to switch gears is context switching, and it creates huge amounts of waste in our days. The American Psychological Association reports that even minor mental blocks created by shifting between tasks can consume as much as 40 percent of someone's productive time. They've also concluded that most of this loss is immune to preparation, meaning that even planned context switching wastes productive time.[2]

Allowing marketers to sit on stable teams that focus on a small number of projects with a shared purpose helps alleviate this depressingly common issue. Our goal in Rimarketing is to design teams that are dedicated to serving a particular customer or audience so we can establish focus and flow and eliminate the waste of context switching.

Finally, execution teams that are organized around a shared goal can effectively balance their day jobs—or their "business as usual" work—with long-term strategic efforts. A large majority of marketers have recurring tasks that are part of their core job description; these make up their day job. In my pre-Agile-coaching days, I was a content marketer, which meant I had to write blog posts, emails, landing pages, etc., all the time. Outside of a Rimarketing environment, most individual contributors are expected to manage this kind of work on their own, usually under the watchful eye of a middle manager. It's independent of larger project work, which would be managed by a project manager inside a tool of some kind.

This separation creates a huge amount of dark work, tasks that nobody sees and that can't be quantified. We don't know the impact dark work has on individual productivity, how much it delays other crucial tasks, or even what percentage of someone's time is devoted to it. Even Agile marketing teams who don't use Rimarketing struggle with this; their tendency is to visualize "big picture" work and

2. American Psychological Association, "Multitasking: Switching Costs," March 20, 2006, https://www.apa.org/research/action/multitask.

apply Agile practices to it while everybody carries on doing their day jobs in whatever way they can manage.

Rimarketing insists that we break down the barrier between business as usual and strategic work for the execution teams. And the team members' shared purpose is a crucial part of this step because it will allow them to determine whether their day jobs are *actually* contributing to their ability to serve the team's purpose. Remember that each execution team should have a core KPI (or maybe two) by which their success gets measured. If I'm a content marketer spending 70 percent of my time writing demand-generation content, but I sit on the retention team whose core KPI is reducing churn, 70 percent of my time is being spent in a way that isn't helping my team succeed.

Or maybe I'm spending that same proportion of time writing upsell emails to existing customers. That's still probably contributing to my team's KPI, but it might be at such a volume that I can't meaningfully contribute to any bigger initiatives. Again, we'll only know this if my business-as-usual work is out in the open, right next to strategic, project-level work.

Freeing Execution Teams to Execute

To guide a group of execution teams, we establish a strategy group. This team ensures that when two or more execution teams need to collaborate, they have a shared vision from which to work. Creating a clear, documented, stable strategy also frees up execution teams to get on with the business of doing great work. They don't need to worry about whether they're doing the right things because that evaluation has already happened.

Strategy groups can also help remove dependencies and impediments that frustrate multiple teams. Strategy groups are true to their name: they create strategies rather than perform actual marketing tasks. They make sure that the execution teams are set up to succeed in *their* efforts to do amazing work. That interaction is difficult to get right, but it's crucial to making Rimarketing work at its highest level. We'll look more closely at the structure of strategy groups and how they interact with execution teams later in this chapter.

The last level of Rimarketing is the leadership team. Smaller teams may not need to establish this group at a formal level, but if you have ten or more full-time marketers, a leadership team will benefit you. This is where year-long strategic objectives are set, critical KPIs are chosen, and, at the enterprise level, interteam and interdivision collaboration gets facilitated. For marketing teams that are accustomed to racing from one campaign to another without an overarching goal, the leadership team is there to help.

Lastly, the leadership team acts as the final arbiter of disagreements between strategy groups. We want to remove empire-building tendencies and leaders' typical focus on completing *their* pet projects. Those unhelpful command-and-control behaviors should be replaced by collaborative, team-centric work designed to meet agreed-on strategic objectives.

But from time to time, even the most well-meaning strategy groups disagree on what work the execution teams should be doing. These conflicts can be healthy, because they surface different perspectives on how to achieve larger goals. But to gain consensus and execute in unison, the leadership team may need to weigh in to maintain alignment when strategy groups clash.

As with the other people-related components of Rimarketing, we'll examine the leadership team and its responsibilities in much more detail. For now, a quick point of clarification: leadership teams aren't evil overlords pushing other teams to do more faster. They are, instead, the gardeners responsible for creating holistic conditions for growth and success for *everyone* who's part of the Rimarketing ecosystem.

Balancing How and What for the Execution Team

Rimarketing execution teams, as we've seen, are responsible for the "how." They consider the objectives, apply their experience and expertise, and decide on the activities they'll undertake to make those objectives reality. Strategy groups, on the other hand, are responsible for the "what." They determine the long-term strategic goals that marketing needs to complete, which should ideally also be tied to larger organizational objectives (see Figure 13).

FIGURE 13
How and What Cycles

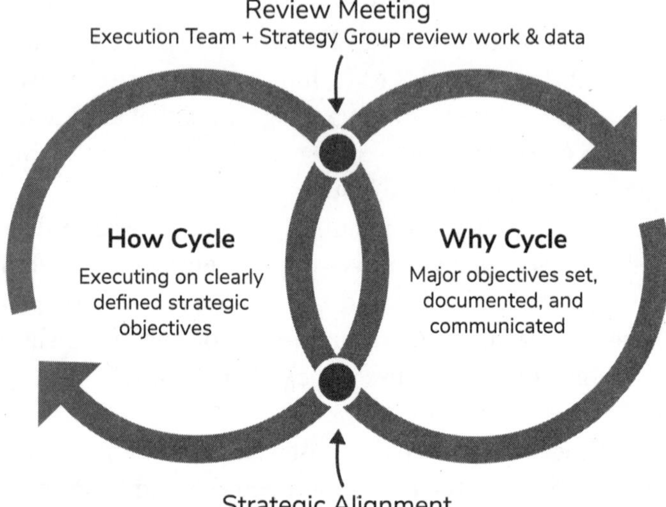

Rimarketing Framework® AgileSherpas.

For this partnership to work effectively, strategy groups need to be comfortable letting go of the how. If representatives from the strategy group don't trust the execution team to get their stuff done right and on time, they'll micromanage the team's members. They'll also slow everything way down by insisting on regular reviews or status updates.

Remember, Rimarketing leaders are gardeners, not plants. They work to ensure that the garden is in the optimal state to produce amazing things. They don't stand over the plants asking to review each bud before it flowers or overanalyzing the symmetry of every leaf. The plants don't have to worry about where to get fertilizer or water, or if they're growing in the right direction, because the gardener sorts all that out. Each half of the partnership has a distinct, but equally valuable, role to play.

With that said, the execution team can, and often should, be incorporated into "what"-level conversations sooner rather than later. Part Three will discuss the process that governs team interactions, and we'll go into a lot more detail there, but for now keep in mind that we want to embody the Rimarketing principle of trust by showing the individual contributors that their opinions are respected. This means inviting them into strategy sessions where they can add value (without falling into the "everyone needs to be in every meeting" trap).

Who's on the Execution Team

The execution team is made up of dedicated individuals who pool their talents to form a cohesive, persistent team. The exact skill sets an execution team needs will vary widely depending on the kind of work they do, but ideally you want within the team all the skills necessary to execute the team's work (also known as being cross-functional, as you'll remember from earlier). In other words, you want to reduce dependencies among different execution teams.

Anytime one execution team relies on another, bottlenecks can emerge and delays ensue. This isn't to say that those issues won't ever crop up when a team has no dependencies, but the fewer opportunities they have for that to happen, the better.

A slightly contradictory mandate for the execution team is to keep it small, ideally between four and ten people, as mentioned earlier. The small size can make creating a cross-functional team challenging if you're working with highly specialized individuals. (This is one of many reasons why we want to develop people into T-shaped marketers.) But it's necessary, because decades of research on group performance has proven that small groups simply work better together. Once a group's size gets into double digits, subteams begin to form (albeit informally), leading to cliquish behavior that undermines the team's ability to perform and eventually eroding their gains.

The execution team's main job is to deliver value to a particular customer, as quantified by their core KPIs. To do so, they need most of their working time available to actually, well, work. That means they need to be kept out of meetings whenever possible because meetings typically don't add value. We can't just magically eliminate meetings, however (at least not all of them), so we concentrate that particular requirement into a single person within the team, which in Rimarketing is known simply as the team lead.

The team lead can have almost any traditional marketing title, but they typically come from the senior managerial level or above. They need at least a moderate level of seniority to effectively navigate organizational politics, and in some corporate cultures to even be allowed in a room with senior leadership. Rimarketing relies heavily on the team lead, so let's see exactly what this person is responsible for:

- **Being a stable point of contact:** Whenever someone outside the execution team needs something from one of its members, they approach the team lead, who incorporates the request into the team's existing priorities and commitments, eliminating hallway conversations or surreptitious requests that can result in context switching for individual contributors and derail the execution team's planned, strategic efforts.
- **Managing temporary SMEs and shared resources:** In even the most well-designed systems, there will be outliers who don't fall precisely into the execution team structure. In marketing groups these tend to be subject-matter experts (SMEs) who have a skill set that's crucial to an execution team's success but isn't always necessary (more on SMEs later). The team lead is responsible for making sure that the right SMEs are available at the right time to support their execution team.
- **Supporting distributed team members:** Another inevitable fact of life for the modern knowledge-worker is that some (or maybe even all) of a team won't work in the same building. We'll discuss processes and practices that help deal with this particular complexity, but when you have a mixed team (some colocated and others distributed), it falls to the team lead to ensure that the environment supports both.
- **Fact-finding and requirements gathering:** An execution team works from a prioritized queue of work. As items make their way to the top, the team lead proactively collects information the team needs in order to start on them. This may mean taking meetings with stakeholders, gathering requirements, or some combination of the two. The most

important thing is that execution team members focus their efforts on *doing* work; the team lead focuses on *enabling* that execution.

- **Interfacing with agencies:** Agency involvement can vary widely depending on the capabilities of a particular execution team, but the team lead should typically act as the liaison between the execution team and the agency. I say "typically" because in some instances an internal SME is better equipped to work with an agency. In those cases the team lead may pass this particular duty off to an individual contributor.

Doing the Right Work at the Right Time

Missing from the above list is the team lead's most important responsibility: ensuring that the team does the right work at the right time. This topic gets its very own section because of the impact, for good or ill, the team lead can have in this arena. The activity that produces the magical right work–right time alignment is prioritizing the team queue, or to-do list. This conveys which pieces of upcoming work are most important (they're at the top), and which aren't (they're at the bottom).

The items at the top of the team queue are crucial to achieving its core goals, and they align with the direction in which marketing as a unit is trying to move. Less important or less time-sensitive work falls to the bottom of the queue, freeing up the team from worrying about when those tasks might become relevant.

As they prioritize tasks, team leads need to make sure the team has all the information necessary to tackle the most important work. Often this means having meetings with stakeholders, collecting requirements, reviewing past projects for performance data that might affect the plans, coordinating interteam dependencies, and more. As you can imagine, these activities easily fill a workweek, especially when we factor in the team lead's necessary participation in the strategy group. This heavy workload means that a team lead should *not* also be asked to perform tasks within the execution team.

Because of this distinction, you may find that existing project managers do well as team leads. Assigning them this role can work, depending on the maturity and performance level of the team they're working with. Project managers typically have the organized approach and the internal connections needed to collect requirements and liaise with stakeholders, but they may lack the strategic perspective necessary to prioritize the queue, as well as the people-wrangling skills required to effectively oversee a fledgling self-organizing execution team.

Marketing director types tend to perform best in this role, although their project-oversight and requirements-gathering skills may be slightly rusty. If you have to choose between project management skills and strategic capabilities in your team lead, favor the latter.

Incorporating Strategic Perspective: Strategy Groups

As we learned earlier, strategy groups are made up of marketing leaders who set larger, longer-term strategic priorities for one or more execution teams. The team lead should straddle both groups, splitting their time between supporting the execution team and coordinating strategic efforts with other team leads within the strategy group.

You may also find individual contributors in the strategy group who *aren't* team leads for any particular team. If you have people whose primary responsibility is to research, document, and analyze marketing strategy, they may not be a useful member of an execution team. Because their efforts happen almost exclusively at the beginning or end of the execution process, they tend to feel idle when they're a full-time member of an execution team. Their time might be better spent focusing exclusively on strategy at a higher level, even potentially providing direction to multiple execution teams. See Figure 14 for more on the structure of strategy groups.

In the smallest departments, the strategy group may spin up and down as needed, often on a quarterly cadence when new strategies are called for. But for departments whose headcount reaches double digits and beyond, the strategy group functions best when it's persistent. This allows it to provide ongoing direction to the execution

FIGURE 14

Leaders Can Be on Multiple Teams

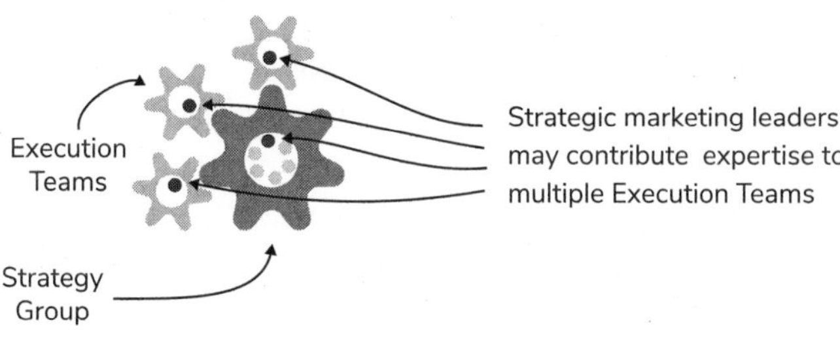
Execution
Teams
Strategy
Group
Strategic marketing leaders
may contribute expertise to
multiple Execution Teams

Rimarketing Framework® AgileSherpas.

teams as questions arise, and to embody the Rimarketing value of adaptability. If, for instance, new competitive data comes to light during the middle of a quarter, an active strategy group will be able to internalize and respond to it in real time, rather than waiting for the next quarterly planning session.

The composition of the strategy group can be tricky for organizations trying to move from a traditional structure to Rimarketing. One team I coached through a transformation struggled deeply with the organizational chart I initially provided, because there were vice presidents, directors, and senior managers sitting together on the strategy group. The VPs also sat on the leadership team, and the CMO was concerned that there was insufficient distinction between the strategy group's members and the function he wanted the group to serve (ensuring that different execution teams were doing the right work at the right time) and the leadership team's mandate (to set and socialize overarching marketing strategy).

We talked through his hesitation, he moved a handful of people around, and eventually we settled on a slightly altered arrangement. The purpose of the two groups hadn't changed, but by aligning their composition more closely with his existing title structure and org chart, he created a step that felt more in line with the way he wanted his senior leaders to be involved with the rest of the marketing function. It was clearly more important to create a step that was powerful without being disruptive, rather than insisting on strict adherence to the design I originally proposed. This, after all, is the essence of the Ri phase.

Teams of Teams, or Forming Packs

When several execution teams come together around a central strategy group, Rimarketing refers to the configuration as a pack. A medium-sized marketing organization may consist of a single pack; a massive group, like the two-thousand-person organization I'm currently working with, will comprise dozens of packs serving many distinct regions, products, business units, or personas.

Like an execution team, a pack needs an overarching reason to exist. It should be clear who's in the pack and who isn't. Each pack requires at least one strategy group—maybe more—to guide the strategic direction of the execution teams that make it up (see Figure 15). Ideally each pack will also have a handful of core KPIs to use in evaluating its performance as a unit.

Packs are similar to the tribes outlined in the Spotify model; the primary distinction is their governance. In Rimarketing, a strategy group helps guide the direction of multiple execution teams to steer the pack in the right direction. The original Spotify model lacks this governing body.

Leadership Teams

Not every Rimarketing department will make use of a leadership team, but if you have more than forty total employees you'll need one. The leadership team sets strategy across the entire marketing func-

FIGURE 15

Rimarketing Packs

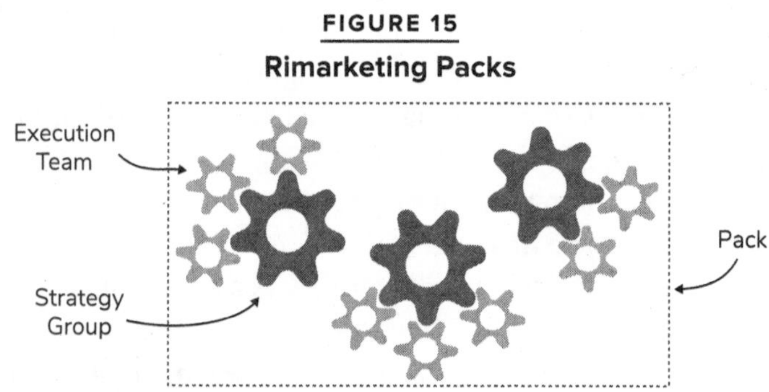

Rimarketing Framework® AgileSherpas.

tion, which it then documents and communicates. Once a department hits this size, you may have multiple packs working on many different kinds of projects and tasks; having a group with a bird's-eye view makes everything flow more smoothly.

The strategy groups review the leadership team's direction and translate it for application within their specific pack. So if we have one pack for North America and one pack for Europe, the Middle East, and Africa (EMEA), the strategy group for North America will take the leadership team's strategy and adjust it to apply more completely to their geographic location. The strategy group for EMEA will do the same.

Or if we have a pack serving the top of the funnel and another working on retention, each of them will determine how their pack will deliver on the leadership team's stated priorities. In this case, some of the leadership team's strategies may not apply to a particular pack. If the leadership team identifies a new audience segment to target, the retention pack isn't going to have a whole lot to do until members of the new segment actually become customers. But even if they won't be working on that segment right away, it's still enormously valuable for them to know about this emerging group and to see how other packs work to connect with it. This insight will allow them to create more cohesive retention efforts when the new segment enters their purview.

Advancing an Agile Career

One of the toughest things about traditional Agile frameworks is their assumption that everyone will be satisfied being an individual contributor almost indefinitely. Scrum, for instance, envisions a perfectly flat team structure with no hierarchy whatsoever. There may be title designations like "senior" or "principal" to indicate seniority or skill, but the structure lacks managers as we typically encounter them in marketing. Even the specialized roles of Scrum Master and Product Owner aren't technically promotions; they're simply different roles.

In Rimarketing, moving from an execution team to a strategy group is sort of akin to getting a promotion, but it's more like a change of state. Instead of being a flower or plant asked to deliver value within a team, you're now asked to create larger systems that enable different plants and flowers to deliver value. In the end the goal is the same: value for the organization and the customers it serves. Promotion or development in Rimarketing is an evolution, and not one that's guaranteed by status or longevity. Moving to different groups signals distinct responsibilities and different capabilities; it's not something that simply happens by virtue of time spent in an organization, or even through demonstrating functional expertise.

Given this flat structure and seeming lack of upward mobility, how do you advance your career in an Agile environment? When there's a single Agile pilot team we can often sidestep this discussion in the short term, but as soon as talk begins of a departmental rollout, the question of professional development and managerial roles must be addressed.

Rimarketing tackles this in three ways: First we have the team leads on the execution teams, whose roles (discussed above) are pivotal. One level removed from that role, we use the strategy group, leadership team, and chapters (see below) to advance marketers' careers. Individual contributors may be asked to leave their execution team and join the strategy group when they reach an appropriate level of seniority to provide the needed departmental, strategic perspective.

Likewise, members of the strategy group can join the leadership team when they're ready to start looking at marketing's role in the larger organization. This move shouldn't be considered "upward," strictly speaking, as we don't diagram Rimarketing teams using typical top-down visualizations. Instead, the transition from execution team to strategy group and from strategy group to leadership team should be considered a move toward the center.

These groups do have more decision-making authority and are likely to undertake duties typically performed at the director level and above. In this way, joining their ranks is akin to a promotion. However, becoming a member of a more central group isn't automatic; it doesn't happen based on how long you've been at the company or how good you are at your functional job. Only when you've demonstrated an ability to think and contribute at the strategic level will you leave your execution team and join a strategy group. Only when you've demonstrated an ability to consider the needs of multiple teams and their roles within the larger organization will you leave a strategy group and join the leadership team.

For individual contributors who excel at their functional role and wish to take on a leadership role, the strategy group isn't the only option. They can also become a chapter lead. Chapters (a term I've borrowed from the Spotify model) encompass groups of people who have the same job but sit on different cross-functional teams. In Rimarketing, this means that members of a chapter come from different execution teams. Chapters take the place of traditional functional teams. They allow people to be supported by colleagues who share similar execution team–level responsibilities, and to have the opportunity to be evaluated by a supervisor who understands what it means to do their job well.

Chapters typically meet weekly, and each one has a lead. The chapter lead is typically the most senior individual contributor in the group; they may or may not also be a team lead on an execution team. Chapter leads are typically where functional managers land when marketing teams move from traditional organizational structures to Agile or Rimarketing. This allows them to maintain some of their professional success while removing the day-to-day responsibility of managing people.

When it comes to reviews, do your best to start moving toward the 360 style as quickly as you can. It's not a requirement for Rimarketing to work, but without it you may have difficulty getting traditional marketing leaders to let go of "their" teams. A detailed explanation of 360 reviews is beyond the scope of this book, but fortunately we have the internet. A quick search for "360 reviews" will point you in the right direction.

In a nutshell, 360 reviews allow you to see a more holistic view of an employee's performance. You get input from team members, managers, other departments, etc., and combine them into a single review. In Rimarketing, this means you'll survey the execution team, the team lead, members of the strategy group, other members of the chapter, the chapter lead, and maybe members of other departments and the leadership team. All that feedback gets combined into a complete, 360-degree look at someone's job performance.

Psychological Safety: The Key to High-Performing Teams

One group I coached had a vice president of creative who struggled to embrace the new Agile ways of working. She was accustomed to reviewing every piece of work that her designers and writers produced, sometimes up to a dozen times, before it reached an audience. What she saw as careful oversight of creative efforts in service of high brand standards came across to others as extreme micromanagement.

The new CMO who spearheaded the Agile transformation suspected that the VP was a departmental bottleneck, but she couldn't be sure. As the Agile pilot began, its team members immediately ran up against the VP's insistence on reviewing every item "her" employees worked on, even though they were now part of the Agile pilot. After a particularly serious event in which she explicitly told the Agile team not to work cross-functionally if it meant circumventing her writers' involvement, the team asked the CMO (and me as their Agile coach) for help.

In the name of empowerment, the CMO told the VP to address the communication issue with the Agile pilot team, and left it to the VP to settle the matter. The VP called a meeting with the Agile pilot team, sat down, and told them to tell her what the problem was. I had coached them in advance to approach the conversation from a place of curiosity and to start by asking questions, but the VP wasn't interested in a chat. She had been told to resolve the communication issue, and her reason for calling the meeting was for the team to tell her what was wrong so she could fix it.

Because the VP held direct control over the professional futures of several of the pilot team members, she could make all their lives difficult. Naturally, they weren't overly excited about telling her how they really felt about her behavior. As you can imagine, it wasn't a very productive meeting.

The next day the CMO expressed frustration to me about the conversation not going well. I told her that a crucial ingredient had been missing that could have made progress possible: psychological safety. Unless teams feel safe asking questions, making observations, and generally speaking up, they cannot excel.

Recall from Part One the definition of psychological safety from Amy Edmondson: it is a "shared belief, held by members of a team, that the group is a safe place for taking risks." It is "a sense of confidence that the team will not embarrass, reject, or punish someone for speaking up. . . . It describes a team climate characterized by interpersonal trust and mutual respect in which people are comfortable being themselves."[3]

The Agile pilot team in this case had been grappling with the VP's micromanagerial tendencies for years. Many of the team members had been punished for perceived (or actual) defiance of her wishes. There was no guarantee that they could speak up in that meeting without repercussions.

Part of the job of strategy groups and leadership teams is to make sure that team members enjoy psychological safety, and that it permeates across the marketing organization. When either of those elements is missing, high performance is impossible. Innovation becomes unlikely, and even the basic efficiencies of Rimarketing are at risk.

Designing Your Perfect Agile Environment

The Agile Manifesto exhorts us to bring together teams made up of motivated individuals, "give them the tools and environment needed to succeed, and trust them to get the job done."[4] A nice general idea, but how do we turn it into reality? What kind of environment is conducive to successfully executing work in an Agile marketing department? Although at every organization idiosyncrasies will come

---

3. Amy Edmondson, "Psychological Safety and Learning in Work Teams," *Administrative Science Quarterly* (June, 1999), 350–383.
4. Agile Manifesto, http://agilemanifesto.org/.

into play, marketing leaders should keep in mind a handful of consistent best practices when putting together Rimarketing teams.

First, come to terms with the fact that colocation and face-to-face interaction deliver far superior results. The trend toward remote work, flexible schedules, and distributed teams have made this sentiment unfashionable in the last five years, but there's no getting around it. A single five-minute conversation can do more to unblock a project than dozens of emails.

Taking a walk around the block together while discussing a new project can reveal solutions that instant messages just couldn't find. And in the world of hyperconnectivity in which most knowledge work happens, we're about a million times more likely to send an email, text, or instant message than we are to actually dial someone's phone number for a chat. Whenever possible, we need Rimarketing teams to be colocated.

But simply being in the same building, or even on the same floor, isn't enough to achieve the full benefits of colocation. If someone sits more than eight feet away from a colleague, the likelihood that they'll get up and go talk to them plummets. You may be unable to easily switch your seating arrangement to overcome this inertia, but you should know that it exists. If your Rimarketing team members sit across a large office from each other, they'll need to work extra hard to create opportunities for face-to-face conversation.

Seat choice may seem like a bonus when your main focus is process improvement, but the impact of physical location is huge. For some pilot teams it can be the make-or-break factor. One group I coached decided to launch a pilot effort, pulling together five people from their forty-person department to experiment with new ways of working. Their operations director found them a nook to move to, and the team began to choose their desks in the new area. Across the department, a longstanding feeling endured (which predated any talk of agility) that the creative team was always given preferential treatment, including the best desks. So when the writer and designer on the team tried to lay claim to the nicest spots, those preexisting resentments began to surface.

Things got very tense very fast, resulting in some serious conversations among the team, myself, and their CMO before the question of physical environment was settled to a reasonable degree of satisfaction. The bottom line: where people sit matters. For some people it's a political or status symbol; for others it's productivity through proximity. Whatever the underlying motivations, don't make the mistake of thinking that environment is irrelevant.

If you can't bring people together physically, your fallback should always be video as the preferred means of virtual conversation. Every team member should have the technology needed to join meetings via video, and this should be the expectation for all members who are not in a room together. The visual cues of facial expression allow us to pick up on subtleties that phones just can't capture. And nothing leads to frustration faster than trying to force complex information to flow through email or instant message.

Being on camera also helps remove the temptation to multitask during meetings, which we've all fallen victim to during our working lives. Knowing that our colleagues can see as well as hear us acts as a great motivator to be engaged, not just dialed in, for meetings.

I work from home when I'm not on-site with clients, so I understand the allure of staying in your pajamas all day. But it's an inescapable fact that face-to-face conversations are powerful and productive. If you don't want to (or can't) go into an office every day, the price is getting on video calls. Make it a habit, and you'll be amazed at the uptick in productivity you enjoy.

Finally, if video is your de facto mode of interaction for one or more execution teams, you need to supplement those digital conversations with actual face time. As we'll discuss in later parts of the book, the quarterly planning session that Rimarketing calls for is an ideal time to bring distributed employees together. Make it an event that team members look forward to, one that's both productive and enjoyable. If you choose not to bring teams together for quarterly planning, create some regular, recurring opportunities for the members to reconnect in real life.

If you've fully adopted the virtual working trend, you may find it challenging to reverse course in the name of marketing agility. Some groups, like IBM and TIAA, have made rejoining an office a condition of employment under the new Agile system, a policy that's led to greater collaboration but also a high level of employee turnover.

Consider this decision in the context of your larger change efforts around Rimarketing. Demanding a return to office life for employees used to the flexibility of remote work might be too much of a stretch. For strong contributors, it's probably not worth pressing the issue while simultaneously demanding major process change. On the other hand, removing the virtual-work crutch that may be propping up some underperformers on your team could be valuable.

Beyond where people sit, consider whether there's physical support for another Rimarketing principle: visibility. Whether it's a wall of sticky notes or a monitor displaying the team's digital tool, everyone needs to have a way to view workflows. If blank walls are hard to come by in your space, you may need to invest in some rolling whiteboards that can go wherever the team needs them. If you're already playing musical desks as you bring people together in new execution teams, take the opportunity to ensure that each execution team has a good area for workflow visualization.

As with enabling face-to-face conversations and natural collaboration, we want to facilitate teams' ability to refer to their boards. The board should be the source of truth, which means people inside and outside the team should be able to actually view it with minimal effort. People will naturally glance at a board that's posted on a wall; they're far less likely to take the time to log in and dig for the information they need.

Changing the physical environment may be a longer play; if it is, redouble your efforts to support the execution teams in the interim through video capabilities and regular get-togethers.

PART 3

PROCESSES
Separating What We Do from How We Do It

We should work on our process, not the outcome of our processes.
If you can't describe what you're doing as a process, you don't know what you're doing.

BOTH QUOTES FROM W. EDWARDS DEMING

PROCESS IS NO LAUGHING matter. I often refer to myself as a process nerd because I'm just as concerned with the *way* things get done as I am with the things I'm doing.

When processes are documented, sustainable, and repeatable, haphazard effort turns into strategic execution. A good process improves every piece of work that flows through it. A bad one can destroy even the most brilliant ideas.

The Rimarketing framework consists of two concurrent and interdependent processes, both of which we've briefly met already: the What Cycle and the How Cycle. The What Cycle is a high-level look at what marketing is trying to accomplish over the long term. It includes yearly initiatives, organizational objectives, new market segments to tackle, major product launches or changes, and the like.

The How Cycle zooms in on these larger goals and breaks them down into their constituent parts. As its name suggests, it covers how marketing will be able to accomplish the lofty agenda to which it's committed. We can also think about the What Cycle as the strategic component of marketing, while the How Cycle covers the tactical execution. The former is governed by the strategy group, and the execution team owns the latter.

The leadership team ensures alignment across the two cycles and also arbitrates any disputes as the cycles interact. The alignment function of the leadership team is particularly crucial in sizable departments where multiple groups need to work together on large initiatives. Rimarketing includes several recurring touch points designed to keep teams in sync, but as projects develop, issues around prioritization, collaboration, and coordination will arise that need an arbitrator. The leadership team plays this role. Their only priority should be ensuring that the execution teams deliver on the departmental and organizational objectives outlined in the What Cycle, so they *should* be an impartial judge in any interteam disputes. They may also simply need to clarify the relative importance or urgency of goals if execution teams have questions.

The larger point here is that in Rimarketing, a leadership team doesn't just create some strategy slides, show them during annual planning, and then disappear. They're responsible for supporting the execution teams throughout their work in the How Cycle.

I've separated the What and How Cycles to achieve a balance between ideas and execution that's lacking in most Agile frameworks. Scrum@Scale gets closest with its Product Owner–and Scrum Master–level cycles, but neither of those roles is common in an Agile marketing environment, so this nomenclature and organizational structure don't translate well into the world of marketing. Ultimately, in marketing the kind of thinking that identifies threats and opportunities is distinct from the kind of thinking needed to figure out how best to mitigate those threats or exploit those opportunities.

Likewise, traditional marketing systems break down when the What group (usually marketing leadership in one manifestation or another) attempts to simultaneously figure out what should be done *and* how it will be achieved. Unable to trust that teams can get things done right and on time, leaders micromanage and hover. Although they do so in the name of meeting deadlines, aligning with brand standards, or other seemingly reasonable motivations, their inability to step back stymies creativity among individual contributors. The teams become short-order cooks, taking orders from higher-ups and losing all sense of autonomy or ownership over their work. Micromanagement strangles innovation, resulting in the all-too-common cycles of burnout and churn. It also illustrates how little regard leaders hold for their teams, and teams know it. They won't be fully engaged in the work because they can tell they aren't *really* in charge of it. To get the fruits of high performance that we discussed earlier, teams need to be empowered to decide how they'll go about achieving the goals established in the What Cycle.

By separating the What and How Cycles, Rimarketing asks one group to think strategically while the other focuses on tactical execution. It allows the execution team to focus on doing amazing work without stressing over whether or not that work is the right thing to do. Execution team members feel trusted to create useful collateral that delivers on stated objectives, and strategy group members have the time and mental space they need to look outward and plot the course to the next big win.

Although the two processes are separate, there's no wall between them; one can't be successful without the other. That means we not only need to establish the activities that make up each cycle; we also have to get clear on how, when, and why the two intersect. Refer back to Figure 13, "How and What Cycles," on page 56.

This part of the book focuses on some best practices for executing the What Cycle. Part Four gets into detail about the How Cycle.

Phase 1 of the What Cycle: The Annual Plan

The What Cycle begins with a very typical marketing meeting: annual planning. However, a crucial difference exists between Agile planning (what we'll use here) and traditional planning (what you'll find in most marketing organizations). Agile plans are well thought out yet flexible. By contrast, most planning activities take place at the point of maximum ignorance, meaning we plan the most during the time when we know the least. Because we haven't done anything yet, there's no indication whether our plans will work. Despite this gap, we usually create elaborate documents filled with dates, requirements, and charts. Surely this will work if the boxes all line up! Plans make us feel productive and safe, but they're typically wrong within hours of completion.

Complex plans can also introduce enormous amounts of waste into a system, because a change in one part of the plan decimates all the carefully calculated steps that follow. For instance, project managers create the always-popular Gantt chart to guide the timing for all the tasks that are required for an upcoming project. But then one of the early tasks gets delayed for some reason, meaning every subsequent date is now wrong. If you're fortunate enough to have a fancy workflow management tool, you might be able to change one date in the project and have the rest update automatically, but many project managers aren't that lucky. They've got to go back to their Gantt chart or project plan and amend every date based on the early change. And then, of course, they've got to talk to all the people affected by the change to let them know that their piece will be delayed.

To put it mildly, this kind of project management is inefficient. It uses up a lot of people's time, making them look very busy without delivering the rapid, customer-centric marketing that audiences expect. It also doesn't reflect the realities of the complex knowledge work we do in marketing. Gantt charts and perfect project plans assume no variability. They're designed to work in a closed system where nothing ever changes. Ever seen a marketing department where nothing changes for months at a time? Yeah, me neither.

In contrast, the objective of the Rimarketing annual plan is not to lay out in minute detail every activity or campaign that marketing will deliver within a year. We can't possibly know that, because we're planning too far ahead, and everything changes all the time. Instead, its purpose is to provide the destination for this year's journey; the path itself will emerge while the work gets done. The Rimarketing annual plan isn't a huge marketing plan. It's a clear, finite set of guiding objectives that the team will refer to as they execute, and that the strategy groups will refer to during planning meetings.

The Rimarketing annual plan should be aligned with the goals and needs of the organization as a whole, but it should focus on how *marketing* plans to contribute to those goals and needs. If one of the overarching goals of a business-to-business (B2B) organization is to increase its software's reach into more departments within the enterprise, marketing's annual plan should articulate how they plan to assist in achieving those goals. Maybe they'll run some experiments to test existing messaging with new audiences. Maybe they'll conduct a content audit to identify assets that can be reused. Maybe they need to craft unique social media strategies for each of the new departments on the roadmap. They could do a lot of different things, but any activities that fail to clearly roll up to organizational priorities need to be strongly justified to make it onto marketing's annual plan. And while the annual plan should be clear, it shouldn't be dictatorial. Remember, the annual plan is part of the What Cycle, so it conveys priorities and objectives, not tactics. Take a look back at Figure 8, "Planning Levels" (page 20), for a visual clue to where the annual plan falls in the overall planning process.

Stakeholders may suggest avenues that they believe will work well based on their experience and expertise, but the final responsibility for deciding how goals will be met lies with the execution teams and their How Cycle.

Additionally, the Rimarketing annual plan will be most effective if it stays focused and small. We'll take a page from the original Agile Manifesto for Software Development here and remind ourselves to maximize the amount of work *not* done. The best strategies focus on removing activities; only then can real progress be made on the remaining items. For best results, try to limit your annual objectives to twice the number of execution teams who'll be executing on that plan. So if you have eight execution teams, you get no more than sixteen annual objectives—and you don't have to use them all! If you only have two execution teams, you get four annual objectives. Again, this doesn't mean you'll only be running four campaigns this year. It means there are only four core goals onto which your campaigns will map.

Annual goals also need to be stable to provide a trustworthy anchor for execution teams and strategy groups. Imagine a strategy group spending days creating lovely plans for all the execution teams they support. The execution teams go off and diligently execute that work for three weeks, reveling in their consistent progress. Then one day they hear that leadership has made a major pivot that's rendered all their work obsolete.

How creative do you think the strategy group will be when crafting their next plan? Will the execution teams work as diligently or delight as fully in their work if they're worried it will all be for nothing? This is why we need consistent guidance at the annual level.

The obvious follow-up question, of course, is what a Rimarketing team should do when there's a major market shift, a new competitor that emerges, or an entirely new channel that explodes onto the scene. As all Agile systems do, Rimarketing systems welcome and plan for change. When there's a competitive advantage to be gained, they stand ready to pounce on change. We should exploit change rather than shy away from it (remember Principle 6: Bias toward Action). The remainder of the Rimarketing planning cycle outlined in this part of the book will show you how to incorporate those seismic shifts in a way that takes maximum advantage with minimal disruption.

But the *source* of the change is key. There's a difference between a fundamental change in market conditions and someone having a cool idea in the shower. One is an externally imposed, unavoidable change. The other will probably turn out to be change for change's sake.

Volatility is unavoidable, and it's one reason that Agile systems and learning organizations are thriving while others are imploding. But it's precisely *because* we can't avoid volatility that we shouldn't introduce it into a system willy-nilly. Proposed changes must come with strong business cases—or risk being dismissed as wasteful, unjustified pivots.

One of the things that has frustrated many teams I've coached is the feeling that they're executing work in the dark (or as I like to say, "If a plan falls in a forest, does anybody follow it?"). Executives and leaders get so far behind (usually because they're busy micromanaging the execution of work) that it's April before they've documented any annual objectives. And once an annual plan exists, the teams aren't sure how long it will be around, or how their daily work is supposed to contribute. In the face of this uncertainty, they copy and paste, doing the same type of work they've always done and playing the waiting game. As you can imagine, such an environment fails to foster innovative, needle-moving, industry-leading work.

A Rimarketing annual plan must be not only stable and timely, but clearly communicated and well socialized. The usual suspects may work well here, namely the annual plan slides that marketing departments everywhere use. Leaders should clearly document their goals and objectives, but they should also show up to answer questions about them. Some of my favorite quotes about Agile planning and documentation come from Jeff Patton, the creator of user stories. Here are a couple:

> Shared documents aren't shared understanding. . . . Shared understanding is when we both understand what the other person is imagining and why.
>
> There are a great number of people who believe that there's some ideal way to document. That, when people read documents and come away with different understandings, it's either the reader's fault or some fault of the document writer. It's neither. The answer is just to stop it. Stop trying to write the perfect document. Go ahead and write something, anything. Then use productive conversations with words and pictures to build shared understanding.[1]

At the end of the day, we don't need the world's clearest, most beautiful planning slides. We need the opportunity for the leadership team and strategy group that created them to talk about them with the execution teams that are responsible for doing the work they call for. Only through discussion (and documentation of that discussion) will the various groups arrive at a shared understanding that will deliver productive work aligned with strategic priorities.

With that in mind, we need to make a few adjustments to traditional annual planning to bring it in line with Rimarketing principles.

Three Adjustments to Your Annual Planning to Make It More Agile

1. Share your slides with execution teams before unveiling the annual plan. We want execution teams to have the opportunity to review the output of the first part of the What Cycle (the annual plan) *before* the meeting with the leadership team and strategy

1. Jeff Patton, "User Story Mapping," JeffPattonAssociates.com, https://www.jpattonassociates.com/read-this-first/.

groups. This way they can see what doesn't make sense and bring intelligent questions, comments, and concerns to the meeting. When people see the plan live for the first time while a marketing executive is talking through it, they can barely process the information, much less formulate feedback on it.

Again, the goal of annual planning in Rimarketing is not a perfect set of slides. It's establishing shared understanding between the leadership team and strategy groups that crafted the strategy and the execution teams that will be executing it. For that to happen, everyone needs to come prepared to discuss things together.

2. Create conditions for collaboration. No judgement implied here, but most annual marketing-planning meetings feature a handful of people talking to a whole bunch of other people who are pretending to listen while actually instant messaging each other ("OMG like we're really going to be able to pull that off [eye roll emoji]") and/or answering email. We schedule this meeting because we're supposed to have it, but few people get any value from it.

In Rimarketing, we want to avoid the typical we talk/you listen dynamic. A Rimarketing annual planning meeting should allow for communication, documentation, and adaptation. That means we need everyone to be heard and seen. If at all possible, get everyone in the same room. If you can't manage that, get larger groups (divisions, packs, etc.) together in their own separate locations and video each location in. Whatever format you use, do *not* have hundreds of anonymous people dialing into a conference line and listening to some VPs talk about slides.

Whether you arrange for some face-to-face time or do the remote video thing, annual planning needs to be well facilitated. You need a designated facilitator who will design the agenda and ensure that people stick to it. One person should be able to manage this if you're face to face; if you have multiple locations you'll need one facilitator per location. If everyone is virtual you can go back to one facilitator, but make sure they're experienced in virtual facilitation and can manage the different needs of this kind of meeting.

You should also have people documenting the discussion, ideally folks who won't be actively participating in it. Give them only the job of reflecting the shared understandings of the group to allow them to focus on this crucial task. If they're *also* trying to participate in the conversation, they may lose the thread and create incomplete documentation.

Per Jeff Patton's recommendation, the products of this meeting should act like vacation photos: we can all look back at them and remember what was going on when they were created. We will refer to them throughout the year to ensure that our daily, weekly, and monthly work is aligned with the initial strategy discussion.

Ideally there should be one final role in the annual planning session, and that's technical support. If you're all in one place you can dispense with this role, but if you have even one person dialing in it's best to have a dedicated role to manage the tech. When large groups connect remotely, you absolutely need someone to handle troubleshooting, test all the software in advance, and otherwise make sure the meeting doesn't get consumed with technical difficulties.

3. Identify metrics and how to measure them. A crucial component of clarity within the annual plan is to identify the metrics and KPIs that will be used to evaluate whether the marketing organization is on track to achieve its stated goals. Explicit phrasing is useful here. Things like, "We'll be successful if we increase X by Y before [date]," or "We aren't achieving success if A is below B on [date]."

Looking at the plan through both lenses—what constitutes success and what indicates failure—isn't something we typically do in marketing, but it's a big part of successful Agile planning. We need to know if the data we're seeing shows a clear win or a definite learning moment so we can act accordingly. Depending on the work being done, we can decide if anything less than success is acceptable—that is, if we fall below the criteria for success but are still above the failure line, how do we proceed? For some projects this might mean we should iterate on the tactics; for others we might determine that anything below true success means we won't proceed with that work. Whatever the approach, it should be clearly and completely documented as part of the annual plan.

Of course, as with all other aspects of the annual Rimarketing plan, the leadership team should be open to feedback from others within the department on what should be measured and where the thresholds for success and failure lie. Per the Rimarketing principle of adaptability, marketing leadership should bring their ideas, but be prepared to adjust them based on feedback during the annual planning session.

Experimenting within the Annual Plan

Any good Rimarketing plan includes some experiments. Not every item should be a known quantity, or there won't be any potential for exponential success, only incremental growth. The Agile marketing team over at CoSchedule, for instance, focuses on doing work that's likely to deliver what they call 10x results. Rather than do standard, safe activities that could deliver a 10 percent uptick in results, they look for ways to get ten times the usual outcome. Of course, they still have to write emails and create content and share on social media, but they've deliberately devised a system that promotes work that has a chance to make a major impact.

Still, experiments in this context aren't crazy, unformed, undocumented wild-goose chases. They need three components to make it into a Rimarketing annual plan: defined hypotheses, measurable outcomes, and clear points at which to pivot or persevere.

1. **Defined hypothesis:** Remember elementary school science? Our understanding of hypotheses has been ingrained in most of us since then, but we've lost track of this vital part of the scientific method somewhere along the way. Any experiment, including a marketing one, is simply a way to test the truth of a statement. Back in elementary school we might have hypothesized, "If I fertilize lima bean plants with compost, they'll grow better than the same type of lima bean plants fertilized with vinegar." Then we'd design an experiment to test that hypothesis. In our marketing lives, we can do the same. A leadership team might ask its execution teams to come up with ideas for improving conversions as part of the annual marketing efforts. One team might surmise, "If we offer customers a thirty-day free trial, they'll convert at a higher rate than if we offer them a seven-day trial." Landing page A/B tests can provide them with quantifiable results to test the veracity of their hypothesis, which will be reported back to

leadership and other execution teams for future iteration. Ideally every annual plan should include at least four of these kinds of experiments so you can run one per quarter.

2. **Measurable outcomes:** Rimarketing aligns with the Agile Marketing Manifesto on this point, which calls for us to value validated learning over opinions and conventions. Gut instinct still matters, but data should be our go-to means of making decisions. To do that well, we need a way to validate our learning from experiments. The lima bean example would require us to measure the height of our plants daily to prove which fertilizer was most effective; our marketing experiments should be just as rigorously monitored. Quantifiable results also prevent experiments from devolving into subjective sniping, with one faction or person advocating for one approach while another advocates for theirs. Even the most experienced marketers guess things wrong, so we should avoid relying exclusively on our guts to guide important decisions.
3. **Clear pivot/persevere points:** The final piece of an effective Rimarketing experiment is a predetermined point (or points) at which we'll evaluate outcomes and decide how (and if) to proceed. Known as a pivot/persevere moment, these are times when we have enough data to determine whether our hypothesis was correct. You'll want to place this moment at least a week after the experiment's start date, but the exact time frame will depend on the kind of test you're running. It can be tempting to jump on seemingly meaningful data before its level reaches statistical significance, but doing so can easily lead to mistakes.

Phase 2 of the What Cycle: The Quarterly Plan

Hot on the heels of the annual plan comes the quarterly plan, in which the strategy groups translate the leadership team's vision from the annual plan into incremental objectives that the execution teams will use to actually get things done. As the name implies, this level of planning is done every three months. You don't necessarily have to do quarterly planning at the start of every quarter; each organization has its own unique cadence, and Rimarketing asks for enough change already. If you typically organize your quarters outside the standard calendar, no need to change that.

The important thing is that plans are in place to cover approximately a three-month period so execution teams have an intermediate goal to work toward. If our annual objective is to travel from New York to Los Angeles, we need to identify a few interim stops along the way.

First, quarterly plans must be tied clearly to annual objectives. If there's a deviation, a substantial amount of time and effort should be devoted to justifying it. Remember that the annual plan contains approximately two objectives per execution team, so it should be fairly straightforward for the teams to turn this directional guidance into chunks of work they can execute in about three months.

One word of caution: don't get too caught up in choosing work that fits *exactly* within the three-month timeframe. Some groups neglect bigger campaigns because some pieces couldn't be completed within the quarter, even though that work might have been a game changer. It's okay for a few items to be left uncompleted and pulled into the next quarterly planning cycle. Likewise, an execution team's quarterly plan should include many projects that are far shorter than three months, because we should be communicating with our audiences continuously, not just when we've collected three months' worth of stuff to show them.

A possible exception to this guideline can occur at the strategy group level. In marketing organizations that serve a large number of products, business units, or personas, individual strategy groups may sometimes have smaller priorities that don't impact groups outside the execution teams they serve. In that case their quarterly plan may contain a small percentage of work that isn't directly tied to annual objectives.

For instance, a fifty-person marketing department I coached was supporting three different pieces of software, each of which was represented by one execution team. The group had overlapping objectives shared between all three teams, but much of their day-to-day activity centered on distinct work to serve their own product. As a result, some of their quarterly activities included tasks that weren't strictly aligned with organizational goals. Despite this, they documented their individual projects with the same degree of rigor to show both why they were going off script and what they planned to achieve by doing so.

With that said, even the most diverse marketing organization needs to clearly establish an acceptable amount of deviation from the larger departmental goals for each execution team. The exact amount will be specific to each group and how spread out the marketing work is, but keep it as low as you can while still allowing strategy groups to own their work. You want to avoid a scenario in which 40 percent of an execution team's work fails to contribute to organizational objectives, but 10–12 percent is probably acceptable. Experimentation is encouraged at the execution team and strategy group levels, but be mindful of the percentage of work being devoted to such efforts. Don't get so caught up in chasing shiny objects that you neglect the tasks needed to keep the lights on.

When it comes to the scope of the quarterly plan, the guidelines are similar to those used during annual planning. Just as leadership teams get to define twice the number of annual objectives as they have execution teams (e.g., six annual objectives for three execution teams), strategy groups have a similar guideline. Since they're looking at shorter time horizons, they'll be working on smaller initiatives. This means they get three to four times the number of quarterly objectives as they have teams. So two execution teams equals six to eight quarterly objectives. If we expand beyond this, the teams have too many balls in the air. To deliver top-notch work on time we must create conditions for focus by maximizing the amount of work *not* done. And, as we've already learned, the more we do at the same time, the longer everything takes.

Marrying What We Do and How We Do It during Quarterly Planning

To create the quarterly plan, we need a special meeting, which marks the formal intersection between the What and How Cycles. This meeting is known as big-room planning (BRP) because it usually takes place with everyone gathered in a large room. Essentially, at this session we want to review and refine the annual plan so it can be effectively executed by a group of teams over the coming three months.

Quarterly BRP is the first intersection of the What and How Cycles, which means we shouldn't rush through it. Here the How people (execution teams) help inform what can realistically be done, provide insight into risks and dependencies, and use their subject-matter expertise to refine goals. The What people (strategy groups and the leadership team) answer questions about big-picture objectives and provide clarification about context and expectations.

One goal of BRP is to get everyone—and I do mean everyone—who'll be working together in a nice big room. Plans are most effective and accurate when the people executing them are involved in their creation, so don't fall prey to the temptation to exclude members of the execution teams from quarterly planning sessions. And since they already have a shared understanding of the annual objectives through the collaborative annual planning meeting, it should be easy for them to successfully take part in BRP.

As with most meetings, especially those with a large number of attendees, BRP can go awry if it lacks clearly stated objectives, a visible agenda, and proper facilitation. To ensure alignment around the goal of BRP, share its objectives with all attendees beforehand. You should also restate the purpose at the start of each day of the meeting and create a visible reminder, such as a poster or whiteboard, to keep everyone focused. Here's a template you can use for your first few BRPs; feel free to adapt it to meet your own needs.

The BRP Agenda

Hat tip to CA Technologies, whose freely shared Big Room Planning agenda informed my thinking on this topic (https://www.ca.com/en/blog-agile-central/planning-agile-part-2-big-room-planning.html).

Prework

Before the actual BRP session begins, team leads, strategy groups, and the leadership team should have done serious preparatory legwork. They should come to BRP with an outline of what they think their team will be doing for the next quarter, including any remain-

BRP Objective Template

Objective: To create alignment among all marketing teams on the goals for the upcoming quarter and how we'll achieve them.

How we get there: By reviewing each team's planned work, we aim to better understand risks, prepare for possible impediments, collaborate more effectively, and be more likely to achieve marketing objectives.

We succeed when:

- each execution team has a clear planning document to guide its work for the quarter
- all other execution teams understand the contents of the planning documents
- sales (and other stakeholders as needed) are informed of the plans for each execution team/pack
- quarterly plans are documented in our project management tool of choice

ing work that didn't get finished from the previous quarter. Team leads may meet together or with stakeholders prior to BRP to ensure they have sufficient information to create plans.

Attendees at BRP will be asked to spend two days crafting their plans for the next three months, which means they can't spend that whole time struggling to understand goals, initiatives, or campaigns. If a new type of work is on the agenda, the leadership team needs to work with the strategy groups to socialize it before BRP begins. In most cases, that means you need an all-hands meeting before BRP begins (be sure it's recorded and that anyone unable to attend watches it). Alternatively, you can spend more time at the beginning of BRP sharing the leadership team's vision and objectives for the quarter, but in a room of a hundred or more people, it's very difficult to engage in a lot of one-way communication. The more you can share up front, the less painful BRP will be.

Day 1

1. Welcome, agenda review, creation of a working agreement (facilitator; fifteen minutes).

2. Share strategic objectives, current progress toward annual goals, provide relevant context for upcoming quarter (leadership team; twenty minutes).
3. Review of upcoming quarterly objectives, events, calendar-centric campaigns, product launches, and anything else that may impact the way teams plan and work for the next quarter (strategy group and/or leadership teams; thirty minutes).
4. Execution teams break out to discuss the impact of #2 and #3 on their existing quarterly plans. Each execution team completes a BRP planning document for their team lead to share with the room; you can find a blank copy at MasteringMarketingAgility.com (execution teams; three-ish hours).
5. Each execution team shares its planning document with the room and answers questions (execution teams and all other attendees; one hour).
6. Following the Q&A session, the execution teams reconvene to revise their BRP documents based on the questions and feedback they received. The leadership team meets separately to discuss any overarching dependencies, concerns, or issues that were raised during the first Q&A (all attendees; until end of day).
7. Leadership may remain for a short session to determine if the plans being laid out align with larger objectives and to discuss any serious risks they need to work on mitigating together. They can also adjust the agenda for Day 2 if needed.

Day 2

1. Review agenda, discuss any outcomes from the leadership session at the end of day 1 (facilitator; thirty minutes).
2. Execution teams reconvene to review leadership input, readouts from other execution teams, and any brain waves team members had overnight. Any new or remaining impediments should be discussed and shared during their final readout. The primary output of this session is an updated planning document (execution teams; two and a half hours).

3. Each execution team shares its planning document with the room and answers questions (execution teams and all other attendees; one hour).
4. If additional dependencies or impediments arise during #3, you may need to repeat #2 and #3 once more (execution teams; three and a half hours, only if needed).
5. When consensus seems close, ask the entire room to indicate how confident they are that the quarterly plan can be achieved. As with all aspects of BRP, aim to get input from the whole group as efficiently as possible. The best way to do so is through an Agile voting method known as "Fist of Five."[2] Once everyone is confident in the plan, BRP concludes.
6. Close with several hours of team socializing.

As you can see, quarterly BRP sessions are very much group activities. Unlike annual planning, which is a What-focused meeting, BRP exists to align the How-focused execution teams with the strategy formulated by the leadership team. For this reason, we get everyone together, unlike at annual planning, when the leadership team can act alone to create the initial planning document. And like the annual planning touchpoint, we want BRP to be collaborative and effectively documented. All the execution teams will use the outputs from this meeting to guide their daily work for three months, so a true shared understanding reflected in solid documentation is key.

If you choose, you may open BRP to nonmarketing attendees, including sales and other internal stakeholders. It can be an ideal time for these groups to get a bird's-eye view of what marketing will be doing over the next three months. The facilitator will document and

---

2. In this voting method, the facilitator makes a statement, in this case something like, "We have all the information and capabilities needed to complete this work and meet our quarterly objectives." Then the facilitator counts to three, at which point everyone raises their hand in the air, holding up one, two, three, four, or five fingers. One finger means they aren't at all confident that the plan is doable, five fingers means they're supremely confident, and so on. If everyone votes three or higher, the plan is approved and BRP is over. If anyone votes a one or two, their concerns need to be voiced and addressed before the session concludes.

Facilitating BRP

BRP sessions can be challenging to get right, especially the first few times you try them. Whenever possible, get an experienced facilitator to help manage the room. You can hire outside professionals to do this (our coaches at AgileSherpas often fill this role for clients), use an internal Agile coach, or ask someone from within the marketing organization who has proven facilitation skills to do it. Wherever you get them, it's vital to have someone keeping people on track, ensuring that the discussion isn't dominated by a few individuals, and maintaining the schedule.

share the outcomes of BRP (it's not a secret meeting, after all), but it can be useful for stakeholders to observe *how* decisions are made about the work that will be done.

You could even invite customers to provide insight into the campaigns being planned. Just be sure that the facilitator knows when these groups are coming and what input they're expected to provide (if any). BRP is crucial to Rimarketing's success, so you don't want to lose time to the sales department derailing the discussion to talk about enablement or customers giving lengthy suggestions that don't match up to the bigger marketing strategy.

The BRP Retrospective

BRP sessions are hard to get right, which means you need to take steps to make each one a little better than the last. Fortunately, there's an Agile practice designed for that exact purpose: the retrospective. We'll go into additional detail in Part Four about using retrospectives at the team level, but here we're concerned about collecting feedback from a much larger group. For best results, you'll want to gather data from attendees immediately following the session, and then supplement it with additional discussion among the team leads and strategy group.

The book *Agile Retrospectives* by Esther Derby and Diana Larsen includes dozens of different activities that you can use to keep the retrospectives fresh as you conduct more and more of them over time, but for your first one you can use the following simple tools to access the wisdom of the group.

Tool #1: ROTI Chart

ROTI stands for "return on time invested," and it simply asks people to share how valuable they found the time they spent on a particular activity. You draw a diagonal line running from the bottom left corner of a whiteboard (or flip chart page, etc.) to the top right corner, and then add labels at regular intervals. The bottom left corner represents a negative return on time invested; people didn't find value in the session. The top right corner is a high return on the time investment, or a very positive net gain. The center represents the break-even point.

As attendees leave, ask them to place a small sticky dot somewhere on the line to represent their own personal return on time invested. If you have a large group, avoid a traffic jam by placing several ROTI charts near the exits and combining the data later.

Tool #2: Stop/Start/Continue

Near the ROTI charts you can designate a spot for more qualitative feedback. Create three columns or large sections on a wall or whiteboard and label them "Stop," "Start," and "Continue." As people leave, they can provide a suggestion under any or all of the categories for the next BRP.

I suggest allowing for anonymous feedback here to capture more honest input; people can have the option to add their name to the card if they're willing to provide more context about their idea.

Tool #3: Leadership Roundup

A day or two after BRP, the leadership team, strategy groups, and facilitator should get together to review the collected feedback and share ideas for future improvements. Don't wait more than a few days to do this; participants' memories are likely to fade quickly.

Based on their own experiences and on input from attendees, the leadership team lists a small set of concrete improvements they'll undertake to enhance the next BRP session. These action items should be documented and shared, along with any trends or standout items collected as part of the feedback process.

A note to marketing leaders: make yourselves available for this and other key Rimarketing sessions. Do not postpone these meetings because some people can't or won't adjust their calendars to attend. Rimarketing meetings happen when they need to happen, and committed Agile leaders need to learn to make time to be there.

What About Recurring Work?

Recurring tasks take up a shocking amount of a marketers' professional life, often to the detriment of larger strategic work that would make a much bigger impact. BRP is designed to manage larger, multiperson projects that span several weeks or months; the daily activities that keep marketing afloat don't come into play. But when 50 to 90 percent of a team's time goes to business-as-usual (BAU) work, they can't afford to ignore it during planning. If they do, they'll overcommit and put all their projects at risk.

So how do we factor in BAU work? We know it takes up a lot of time, but most people can rarely provide an accurate percentage. There are two ways to handle this information gap. The first, and best, is to have each marketer keep a time log for a week or two. Don't worry—they don't have to get super granular and go down to the minute. All we're looking for is a rough estimate of how much time is *really* available for the larger projects that will form the topics at BRP. If one individual contributes to different types of BAU work (content creation and social media maintenance, for instance), they should log

TABLE 2

Time-Tracking Table

Monday	Tuesday	Wednesday	Thursday	Friday	Totals
2 hours content	0 hours content	3 hours content	1 hour content	2 hours content	8 hours
.5 hours social media	2 hours social media	.5 hours social media	1.5 hours social media	.5 hours social media	5 hours

those as two separate BAU entries. This isn't a massive undertaking; all you need is a simple log like the one shown in Table 2.

Then combine individual logs to determine how much of a team's time is actually free for project work. When team members come to BRP, they'll be armed with enough information to make realistic commitments based on their recurring tasks. If a team usually spends 70 percent of their collective time on BAU work, they should only take on work to fill the remaining 30 percent and no more, no matter how cool the project or how urgent the problem that comes up at BRP.

A bonus outcome of this lightweight tracking is that it often reveals previously unknown quantities of BAU work. Some teams discover they're spending over 90 percent of their day on the hamster wheel. They're busy all the time, but it's basically just running to stay in place. If this is the case, it'll be up to the strategy groups and leadership team to cut down on the volume of BAU work consuming teams' time. That might mean creating more automated systems, auditing the type of work being done, or eliminating some tasks entirely.

In many teams I've coached, marketers spend hours per week on recurring tasks they believe are essential, only to discover that marketing leadership long ago deprioritized those activities and assumed that the decision had trickled down the org chart. Obviously these are broken systems, and visibility can help fix them. The Rimarketing principle of radical transparency means we'd rather know what people are doing and help them make better choices that lead to better outcomes for everyone. Again, we're looking for ways to maximize the amount of work *not* done in order to create focus for teams and individuals.

Quarterly Planning Meetings with Remote Attendees

Whenever possible we want to get people face to face for BRP. It's only four times per year, so fly people in and turn it into a fun and productive week for the department.

I'd like to stop this section right there, because getting people together is one of the most powerful ways to catalyze teams and achieve previously impossible things. But I realize that the prescription is more realistic for some groups than others, so if you *really* can't get everyone in the same physical room for BRP, avail yourself of a good alternative.

Remote teams can undertake the same planning, sharing, and revision activities as everyone else; they just do it via video. Video is crucial here; don't even try to do this with only a phone line. If the remote attendees can't see what's going on, and if the in-room attendees can't see them sharing, it's not even worth the time for remote people to dial in. If your remote teams aren't all together in one location, they can video in separately. But again, whenever possible, we want to get groups face to face. If remote people are typically spread out, try to collect them together in one location for BRP, even if it's in a different location from the rest of the group.

Good facilitation is key to all BRP meetings, but it's even more important when there are remote attendees. Let your facilitator know in advance if you'll have people attending virtually, and make sure you have the technical capabilities tested well before the session is scheduled to begin. Troubleshooting video for twenty minutes is a bad way to start the time together.

Finally, try to avoid activities that will include in-person attendees and exclude the remote folks. You may even want to bring in a second facilitator whose only job is incorporating remote attendees into the discussions and activities. Any ice breakers or consensus creators should be chosen to accommodate everyone. Likewise, if you spend the last half day of BRP on a team-building or social activity like bowling or axe throwing (that's totally a thing), give the remote team members some opportunity to team build as well. If the remote people are all together, they should do a similar activity as a group. Then each group can share photos of their separate team-building moments with the follow-up documents from the meeting.

Don't forgo fun team activities if you have just a few remote attendees for BRP, but be mindful of any feelings of exclusion that might ensue. Think about how your remote folks may feel if at the next meeting everyone is laughing about the axe mishaps that they couldn't be part of. A lack of complete colocation during BRP isn't a deal breaker, for either the meeting or its social components. But the exclusion factor is just one more argument for getting *everyone* together whenever possible.

Strategic Execution after Quarterly Planning

Some of the most angst-filled questions that arise during any kind of Agile transformation come from middle management. Accustomed to reviewing most of the work their subordinates do and attending meeting after meeting, they find themselves adrift in the team-empowered Agile environment, which is mostly free of status meetings. However, team leads (often former middle managers) and other members of the strategy group have no shortage of work to do after BRP. The work will, in many cases, be substantially different from their previous day-to-day tasks, but it's also more rewarding and impactful. See Table 3 for a summary of how the team lead's responsibilities differ from those of a traditional marketing manager.

The first essential task of the strategy group is to transform the planning document created by their execution team into one or more

TABLE 3

From Middle Manager to Team Lead

Traditional Marketing Manager	Rimarketing Team Lead
Tells direct reports what to do, when to do it, and whether they're doing it right.	Doesn't dictate daily activities. Trusts the team to get things done.
Understands marketing priorities, but may not actively communicate them to the team.	Shows the team what's important by prioritizing their to-do list (queue).
Ensures that all their employees are always productive and busy. Sees downtime as a problem to be solved with more work.	Allows the team to self-organize and get work done as they see fit. Embraces slack and downtime as positive outcomes of a high-functioning system.
Evaluated on whether they "hit their numbers" (e.g., generating leads). Focused specifically on having people do things that deliver those results.	Evaluated on the team doing the right work at the right time. Focused on team activities that deliver value to the target customer or audience.
Typically the bottleneck for things getting released because they need oversight of all work done by the team.	Actively works to push decision-making capabilities down into the team so they aren't delaying work.

FIGURE 16

Strategy Group Cycle

Rimarketing Framework® AgileSherpas.

queues. Analogous to a typical Agile backlog, the queue provides direction for the execution team as they begin their day-to-day work. We'll cover queue functionality and best practices in Part Four; for now it's enough to note that the strategy group needs to take the high-level, quarterly vision for the teams they work with and translate it into an actionable, prioritized list of projects (see Figure 16).

Once work begins, the strategy group will connect with representatives from the execution team to ensure that the team's work continues to align with its KPIs. In a highly interconnected pack where the execution teams must work closely to deliver a final marketing product, this job can take quite a lot of time. The strategy group will also attend smaller planning meetings and reviews with individual execution teams to ask clarifying questions about priorities, see the preliminary results of projects and campaigns, and adjust short-term goals based on initial feedback. As we'll see shortly, the execution team determines how often they'd like this kind of input from the strategy group. But, particularly for strategy groups who serve multiple teams, there will be plenty of touch point requests to fill their days.

In addition to connecting directly with the execution teams they serve, strategy groups will also act as liaison between individual teams and marketing leadership in the form of the leadership team. Any large-scale problems plaguing multiple execution teams, any major directional data coming in, or any new customer insights an execution team gains will be escalated to the leadership level by the strategy group.

One of the most crucial functions of the strategy group is to act as a filter for ad hoc requests being made of the execution teams they serve. Regardless of how effective a BRP session is, new ideas, insights, and input will always come up during a quarter. Rather than have these slide sideways into a team's workflow via hallway conversations or through a casual "hey could you help me with this" email, the strategy group becomes a stable point of contact for all incoming requests to its teams.

To be clear, this doesn't mean that no one can speak to an individual contributor directly. It doesn't mean two people can't get together for an impromptu brainstorming session. It means that individuals cannot be sidetracked from their agreed-on objectives to help with random, unplanned projects. These minor side gigs seem like no big deal, but jumping back and forth among several of them while trying to balance team commitments is a recipe for confusion and delay (not to mention long hours). For this reason (and many others that we'll get into later), any requests for the team or its members need to go through the strategy group. They can then make prioritization calls, weighing the newest ask or idea against existing commitments and deciding which is actually most likely to deliver on the team's KPIs as well as organizational objectives.

The final job that keeps strategy groups busy after BRP concludes (especially during the early days of a Rimarketing transformation) is helping individuals balance their recurring work against the strategic needs that were identified during the BRP session. As discussed before, every marketer has a list of things they do to keep the ship afloat. It will be up to the strategy group to help everyone feel comfortable sharing how they spend their time so that informed trade-offs can be made. It's impossible to work on a dozen things simultaneously; only by maximizing the amount of work *not* done can we truly become productive and efficient. Strategy groups should be the champions of this mindset. They help individuals identify non-value-adding activities and then work to eliminate or automate them (and of course they don't judge the individual for engaging in those activities in the first place).

Marketing Leadership's Role in Executing Quarterly Work

It's not just the strategy group that keeps busy after BRP concludes. The leadership team should stay active between these quarterly touch points as well. Like the strategy group, they may attend planning meetings held by the execution teams or the packs to ask clarifying questions about the work being done, answer questions from the teams about strategic priorities, and adjust those priorities based on input from teams.

The leadership team members are the gardeners of Rimarketing; they work to create conditions in which all the plants can thrive. This means they need to become experts in the environment as well as the audience. After all, we can grow all the peppers we want, but if everybody wants blueberries we're out of luck. The leadership team won't get down in the dirt and interfere with an execution team's activities, but they will be supportive observers of team-level work. And any larger garden-level impediments that arise will hold their attention right away.

Process Nerds Unite: How Work Gets Done in an Agile Marketing System

The next part of the book, "Practices," will concentrate heavily on the activities of the execution team and its work within the How Cycle. Our discussion of process for execution teams at this point will focus almost exclusively on the way they interact with the What Cycle.

Like the What Cycle, the How Cycle resets during each BRP session. All execution teams and their members attend the BRP meeting to provide the appropriate background and context for the work being proposed. After BRP concludes, the interface between What and How is confined to designated representatives, the team leads, to maximize the focus of individual contributors.

Once the strategy group has translated the execution team's planning document into its queue and prioritized it, it's time for the execution team to get to work. They meet with one another every day in a fifteen-minute standup (more on this later), and they meet with the strategy group on a schedule of their choosing. Some execution teams will want to check in with leadership often, particularly if they're a younger team or are tackling new kinds of work. Others don't need much oversight and may only touch base with the strategy group every month.

Execution teams that work closely with one another, either within a formal pack or as informal collaborative groups, may choose to meet deliberately on a regular basis. Planning meetings are often an obvious time for execution teams to intersect, particularly if dependencies are likely to arise in the near future. Execution teams may also attend one another's demo meetings (more on these in the next part of the book) to learn what's been completed recently.

Teams may also find that ad hoc sessions take place among individual contributors and eliminate the need for additional scheduled meetings. As we learned in Part Two, creating an environment that fosters collaboration can be an effective balm to the meeting burnout that most marketers suffer from. Whether or not a group of execution teams has a recurring meeting, a large collection of execution teams that form an official pack (meaning they share a meaningful reason to work together) should get together on a monthly basis to conduct a group planning session (see Figure 17). This ensures

FIGURE 17

Pack Cycle

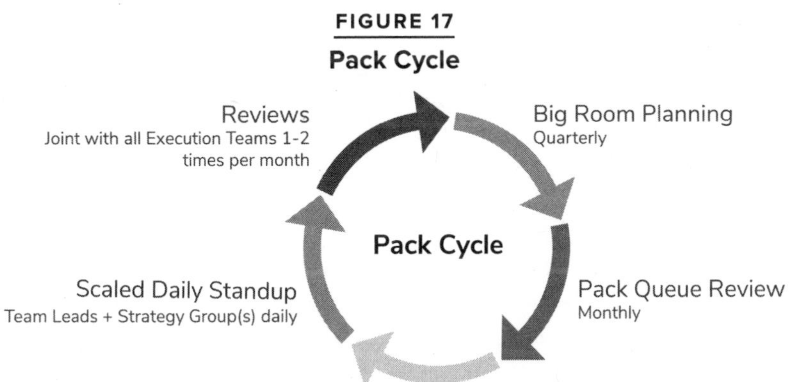

Rimarketing Framework® AgileSherpas.

alignment around their shared goals and allows for new information to rapidly disseminate among the execution teams.

Strategy groups attend all formal How Cycle meetings, escalating any significant threats, learnings, or opportunities to the leadership team as appropriate. Outside of BRP and its preparatory activities, What and How remain complementary, but largely independent.

PART 4

PRACTICES
Daily Activities for Achieving Lasting Agility

Productivity is never an accident. It is always the result of a commitment to excellence, intelligent planning, and focused effort.

PAUL J. MEYER

WHEN I WAS WRITING this book, it was hard—*really* hard—to avoid jumping straight to this material. The specific team-level practices described here hold the keys to so much amazing transformation that I wanted to write about it right away. I have, however, a very good reason for writing about practices last. Practices are powerful, but without the other supporting components their impact will be severely limited.

I see it all the time in teams trying to adopt Agile ways of working. They want a change, so they start implementing some of the simpler practices they know about from Agile. Usually that means putting some stuff on a board, and maybe having daily standup meetings (fifteen-minute check-ins that usually happen first thing in the morning). The problem is that they haven't tried to approach their work from a different perspective. They haven't changed their mindset; they haven't adopted new shared principles; they don't even understand *why* teams take the time to visualize their work on a board or talk together for fifteen minutes every day.

Without the infrastructure behind them, the practices don't seem to work. The board gets cluttered, nobody updates their cards, people start feeling resentful that *another* tool has been foisted on them, and eventually its use dies out. Or daily standup starts off strong, but then people realize they don't really work that closely with some of their teammates, so they stop paying attention to those people's updates. Pretty soon the meeting becomes a rote status report resented by its attendees, and again the practice withers away.

These sad deteriorations are not only frustrating and a waste of the team's time; they can also sour large groups of people on agility in general. "We tried that Agile thing," they'll sometimes tell me, "and it just didn't work."

What they really tried was bolting a handful of Agile practices onto an otherwise traditional system. That's ineffective in the long run, and it's not what anybody wants for their work life. So yes, the practices are the shiny manifestation that makes everyone ooh and aah. But as we discussed in the early pages of the book, even the sexiest-looking car disappoints without a good engine. Take the time to build a good Rimarketing engine. You may be able to do that simultaneously as you adopt some of the practices from this part of the book, but don't try to get by with practices alone. Your car might look cool, but it won't get you anywhere.

Practical Advice for Agile Marketing Teams

Most of the practices in this chapter focus on the execution team, because that's where the daily magic happens in Rimarketing. As you'll recall from Part Three, the execution teams are responsible for the How part of Rimarketing. Most of the What Cycle is completed during annual and quarterly planning activities; the rest syncs up with the schedule established by the execution teams, what I call the Execution Team Cycle (see Figure 18).

If you've been part of an Agile environment, some of what's covered in this part of the book may sound a bit familiar. I'm borrowing practices, activities, and in some cases cadences from existing Agile frameworks like Scrum and Kanban, and I want to fully acknowledge the debt Rimarketing owes to these early incarnations of agility. However, what I'm proposing here is a new iteration of the Agile framework: the Ri version. It builds on, and yet breaks away from, existing options.

FIGURE 18

Execution Team Cycle

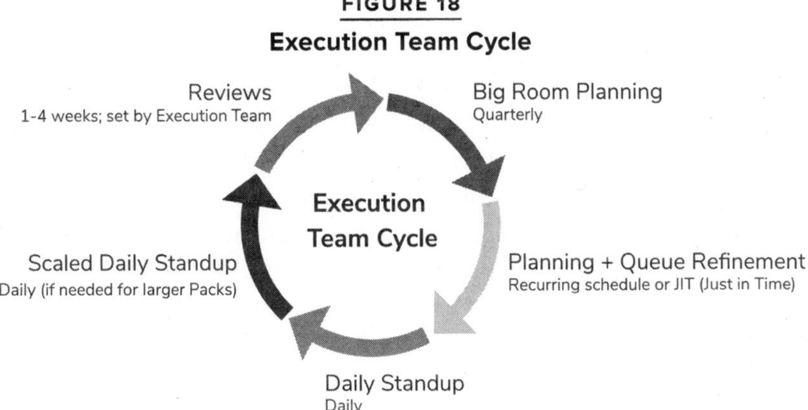

Rimarketing Framework® AgileSherpas.

FIGURE 19

Flow + Iteration

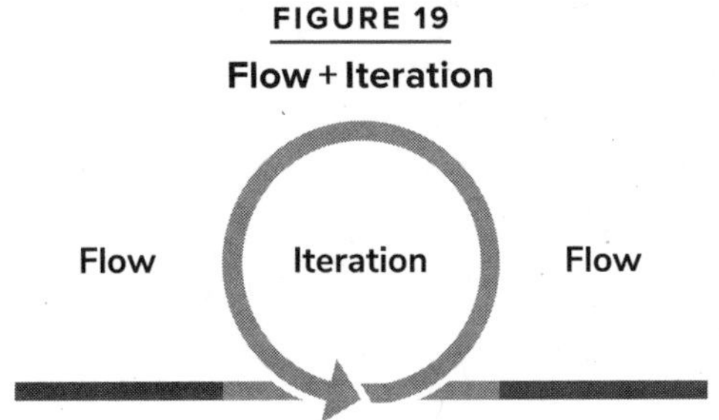

Rimarketing Framework® AgileSherpas.

Let's start by establishing the cornerstone of the Execution Team's How Cycle: choosing between flow and iteration (see Figure 19).

Rimarketing execution teams have the flexibility to decide on the precise mechanism they want to use to manage their work, choosing from these two options. When a team is in flow they're working and delivering continuously without reference to any particular timebox. This is the default operating mode for a Rimarketing execution team. But at times they will need to create focus on a subset of the work in their queue. In these moments they begin a series of iterations, which will last until the identified subset of work is done. An execution team may choose to conduct a single iteration before returning to flow, or they may need several consecutive iterations.

Before Beginning Flow: Visualizing Work

Before a team can begin managing work within either the flow or iteration state, it must first visualize the way that work gets done. Creating visibility aligns with the Rimarketing principle of radical transparency, and it also allows the team to gain insight into what *really* happens as they attempt to complete various pieces of work.

Making the progress of work more visible doesn't have to be enormously complicated; kanban boards will be our tool of choice because they're simple to create and yet convey huge amounts of information (see Figure 20). Tools like Trello have made this kind of visualization very common, so chances are you've seen something like it at one time or another.

While they are simple in theory, kanban boards are also easy to get wrong if you don't understand the guiding principles behind their configuration. First, a good board is an information radiator, which means it provides a lot of insight in a small space *without* making the observer do a lot of mental work to understand it.

Next, the board is very much a team artifact. Team members are the ones who decide how it should be set up. But it will also help

FIGURE 20

Kanban Board

Queue	Copy	Design	Publish	Done

Rimarketing Framework® AgileSherpas.

stakeholders, other teams, agencies—and anybody else concerned with what the team is doing—understand what's going on. A quick review of a kanban board should tell a complete story of what work is in progress, what's gotten stuck, and what's been completed.

You'll notice that the board illustrated above, while simple, has moved beyond a single "In Progress" column, and that is deliberate. The sooner you can get more specific about what's actually happening while work is "in progress," the better. Most marketing projects have multiple phases; they need help from copy, design, email, social, automation, etc. So if all we have is a single progress column, a piece of work could hang out there for weeks. Then we don't know which stages of work are taking a long time and which ones the team is flying through. Without this insight we can't intelligently cross-train people, make the case for hiring additional resources, accurately predict delivery of work, or address bottlenecks in the workflow.

On the other hand, you don't want a board that's overly complicated. If you find yourself with more than ten columns, take a hard look and see if they're all providing important insight. If so, that's great, but don't let your board balloon to a massive width. You need to walk a fine line between a board that's detailed enough to provide insight into the individual phases of work and general enough to function well for the tasks a team is responsible for.

Speaking of avoiding overcomplicating things, each execution team should have only one kanban board. A team might be tempted to create a board for each project or each person, or to place strategic campaigns on one board and business-as-usual work on another. But splitting things up in this way provides only a fragmented view of what's going on with the team. And making intelligent tradeoffs is hard when you can't see all the work side by side. Remember, in order to enhance focus and limit the pernicious practice of context switching, we have to maximize the amount of work *not* done. The only way to do that is to get a holistic, complete view of the team's activities.

If you need to break down your visualization into different components, there are ways to do so without splitting into multiple kanban boards. Horizontal divisions, also known as swimlanes, deliver

FIGURE 21

Kanban Board + Swimlanes

Queue	Copy	Design	Publish	Publish Ready	Done
	Initiative 1				
	Initative 2				
	Initiative 3				

Rimarketing Framework® AgileSherpas.

greater detail on certain aspects of work without requiring a new board. Figure 21 contains an example.

Swimlanes may represent different projects, strategic initiatives, kinds of work, or even people. Their labels depend on what additional information the team or its stakeholders need to glean from the kanban board.

Every execution team needs to visualize its work, but not all kanban boards will look the same. As with all aspects of a Rimarketing system, we're committed to continuous improvement. Your first board design isn't likely to be the best version, so be prepared to iterate on it over time.

One final note: in the spirit of entrepreneurial behavior, each team member is responsible for updating the board with their current activities. If I start a new work item, I'm the one who moves it out of the queue. If my item gets blocked, I'm the one who adds a marker to indicate that status. The team lead doesn't own the board; it belongs to the team, and they should care for it and its contents.

Tools for Visualizing Work

Because an initial board layout isn't going to be perfect, I recommend using a physical kanban board for your first few tries if at all possible.

If most of your team is in the same location, find a wall or whiteboard somewhere, and make it the new home of your kanban board. Even if you have a handful of remote employees, you can still use a physical board. Each remote employee just needs a board buddy who moves their cards for them. The remote person sends an instant message to their buddy, who moves the card the next time they're at the board.

If you're mostly distributed, however, a physical board may not be feasible. In that case, go for the simplest tool that will still deliver your team's early board goals. If vertical columns are all you need, Trello may be your best bet. As of this writing it's easy to get a free board up and running, and it includes useful features like adding members, due dates, checklists, color coding, and other helpful ways to keep the team organized. If you think you'll need swimlanes soon, however, Trello doesn't currently offer that functionality. A more formal Kanban tool will be the way to go.

What you *don't* want is to shell out a ton of money for a fancy project management tool (even if it's an Agile one) before you truly know what you need. Lots of great options exist (Aprimo, CoSchedule, Workfront, and Wrike are currently trying to serve the Agile marketing audience, and the space is really taking off), but until you know your requirements you won't be a very intelligent software buyer. If you can get started in an analog way (or by using a simple free option), you'll learn a lot about your workflow needs very quickly. Then, after a couple of months, you can explore the market with a more informed eye. You'll be far more likely to buy a tool that really helps you, rather than getting one up front and trying to force the team to conform to it.

Creating Focused Effort with Work-in-Progress Limits

The final component of an effective workflow visualization is one of the most simple, counterintuitive, and powerful Agile practices: work-in-progress (WIP) limits. In every workshop I run we do at least one exercise to demonstrate the power of WIP limits, because in all honesty they sound like a ridiculous concept if you're unfamiliar with them. Their guiding principle is that by doing less at any given time, we can ultimately accomplish more.

Most of us believe that the sooner we start on something the sooner we'll finish it, but study after study has proven this common assumption wrong. In fact, the more things we're working on at any one time, the longer all those items take. If I have twenty things to accomplish this week, I may feel very productive if I start them all on Monday. I can also tell the ten stakeholders that I'm working on their project, which should make them happy with me. The problem is, when Friday afternoon rolls around, none of those twenty items will be anywhere close to finished.

If I continue to try to tackle all twenty simultaneously, I may need another full week (or more!) to complete them. I've been jumping back and forth between twenty tasks, which means I haven't had much time to devote to any of them. I've also wasted huge chunks of time trying to force my brain to switch gears and think about different projects. Our brains crave focus and completion; they don't like all those jumps. As discussed in Part Two, context switching is the price we pay for task hopping.

The simplest way for me to accomplish all twenty to-dos is to work on only a few at a time. I tried to finish twenty tasks in five working days, but it actually took me ten days. My lead time for twenty items was therefore ten days. To reduce that lead time to the five days I originally planned for, all I have to do is cut my WIP in half. So rather than trying to do twenty items at the same time, I'll work on ten until they're done and then move on to the next ten. This means that the second half of the tasks won't get started right away, which can be hard for stakeholders to stomach. They want to believe that I'm working on their project RIGHT NOW. But in fact, they'll get it much sooner if I focus on fewer projects at a time.

As you can imagine, this kind of focused effort means that we need a high degree of confidence that we're doing the right work first. (We'll get into the practices for queue creation and refinement shortly.) Data are all well and good, but there's nothing quite like a real-life experiment to drive things home—especially when the concept is as counterintuitive as this one. If you or anyone around you is still skeptical about why or how WIP limits work, try the following quick exercise. In both rounds you will execute the same task: writing the sentence "I will limit work in progress" several times.

Round 1: No Limit on WIP

In this round we'll operate in a traditional model: working on lots of things at the same time. To make the experiment as realistic as possible, think about how many projects you're currently working on, and use that as the number of sentences to write. If you're miraculously not working on a bunch of projects right now, you can use the number five.

When we have no limit on our WIP, we jump from project to project, so in this round you'll write one letter per sentence before moving on to the next. If five is your number, you'll write "I" five times because it's the first letter in the sentence. Then you'll write "w" five times, once in each sentence. Then "i," and so on until you've finished them all. Time yourself, and note when you finish one sentence as well as when you finish all five (or whatever your number is).

Round 2: WIP Limits in Play

Now let's do the same experiment with a WIP limit of one. In this case, you'll work on one "project" until it's completed. For our purposes that means you'll write one sentence until it's finished, and then move on to the next, and so forth until all five (or whatever your number is) are done. Again, time how long it takes you to finish one sentence as well as all five.

It's counterintuitive but true. Limit your work in progress, and you'll accomplish more in less time.

Basic Best Practices for Wip Limits

Limiting work in progress is one of the most powerful ways to complete more work in less time, and there are several different ways to do it. Depending on your team size, specialization, and board design, you may find it helpful to limit WIP in one (or more) of the following ways:

- by person
- board-wide
- by column
- by individual cell

If you have individual contributors with specialized skills who don't do much collaboration or engage in many handoffs, limiting WIP on a per-person basis may be all you need to do. In this case each person agrees to work on only a small number of items at a time, and they'll keep themselves and one another accountable through the team's kanban board. They may even use the simplest form of visualization, with columns for just Queue, In Progress, and Done, because each person's workflow varies too much to allow for further details about what "in progress" really means. A team of five might appear to have a lot of work in progress, but a low per-person WIP limit will keep things moving. If you're using individual WIP limits like this, keep them really low. Two per person is a good starting point, and three is about as high as you can go without dulling the impact of the limit.

If per-person WIP limits seem too granular (or too much like micromanagement), you can create limits that govern the entire board. This works best if the board is fairly simple—that is, with a maximum of two or three active columns. For example, a team of five whose board includes Queue, Creation, Publishing, and Done might establish a WIP of eleven for the whole board. Sometimes there might be eight items in Creation and three in Publishing. At other times Publishing might hold most of the work. The idea here is to give the team flexibility around where the work falls while still creating a system that helps work flow quickly.

The board-based WIP limit works best when you aren't concerned about finding or mitigating bottlenecks in the system (or if you have a very simple system). Since the system is flexible about what stage work is in, you won't be able to see if work is stalling out at a particular stage or with a particular person. Sometimes that's okay; at other times you'll need more specific WIP limits to help uncover issues that need attention.

One of the more specific ways to regulate work in progress is through the traditional use of WIP limits based on columns on a kanban board. Here we set the maximum number of items to be worked on for each stage. So if our board's columns are Queue, Copy, Design, Publish, and Done, each of those phases (except Queue and Done) would have its own unique WIP limit. This approach lets us manage

FIGURE 22

Kanban Board without WIP Limits

Rimarketing Framework® AgileSherpas.

workflow in a much more focused way, because we can dial the limits up or down based on the phase of work. So if our board without any WIP limits looks like Figure 22 much of the time, it becomes clear that we need different WIP limits for different phases.

The phases with less overwhelming volume can get a lower initial limit, maybe just two, while the ones that are always overloaded will need to be higher, maybe five for Copy and three for Design (see Figure 23).

Finally, we can go even further with this column-based WIP limit if we're using swimlanes in our workflow visualization. When we add these horizontal dividers, we create cells on the board, each of which can get its own WIP limit. Taking our previous example, we might add horizontal lanes for three separate initiatives. This means we can establish distinct WIP limits for each phase *and* each initiative, as illustrated in Figure 24. Doing so helps ensure that the team focuses the right amount of work on each subset of activity.

Initiative 1 might be the most valuable and might deserve most of the team's time, but they can't neglect the other two. In this case they'd establish a higher WIP for all the cells in the Initiative 1 lane. They get the benefits of achieving more in less time through the WIP approach, but they also create additional focus on completing the most impactful work. And if a new threat or opportunity arises

FIGURE 23

Kanban Board + WIP Limits

Rimarketing Framework® AgileSherpas.

FIGURE 24

Cell-Level WIP Limits

Backlog	Creation	Editing	Done	Ready	PEN
	Initiative 1 WIP: 3	WIP: 3	WIP: 3	WIP: 3	
	Initiative 2 WIP: 2	WIP: 2	WIP: 2	WIP: 2	
	Inivitiative 3 WIP: 1	WIP: 1	WIP: 1	WIP: 1	

Rimarketing Framework® AgileSherpas.

around one of the other initiatives, they can always adjust the various limits temporarily or permanently to reallocate their work.

Two final notes on WIP limits and best practices: your WIP limits should be painful, and you probably won't get them right the first time.

First, to achieve their goal of helping you stop starting and start finishing, WIP limits need to be set as low as possible while still keeping the team moving forward. A WIP limit that doesn't actually limit work isn't doing its job. On my personal kanban board I have a strict in-progress limit of two, and I bump up against it practically every day. Time and again I'd like to start on a new task, but I'm already working on two. Per my WIP-limit rule, I must finish one of the tasks before beginning another. It's irksome but effective.

A good rule of thumb is to start your WIP limit a bit higher than it probably should be and work your way down. You can try an initial WIP limit of twice the number of people who can work on that task. For example, I'm the only one who can perform the tasks displayed on my personal board, so my WIP limit is two times one, or two.

As with all facets of the Rimarketing system, be prepared to test, learn, and iterate around WIP limits. If you're new to the idea, you won't do it perfectly on your first try, but WIP limits will become a powerful productivity tool if you keep them in place and adjust them until the team is constantly cranking work out.

Advanced Visualization Techniques: Buffers and Pens

As you grow more comfortable using your board, chances are you'll find areas where you need some additional strategies for making work flow smoothly through the system. When that happens, you can explore two advanced options for visualizing work: buffers and pens.

Buffers are most useful once you've identified the bottlenecks in your system. A useful way to mitigate a bottleneck is to ensure that every team member always has valuable work to do, which is where the buffer comes in. A buffer column doesn't have a WIP limit, and tasks placed there aren't actually being worked on. They are simply hanging out, ready to move into the next phase of work.

For instance, if publishing work is the bottleneck of our execution team, we need to make sure there's always work ready for the publishing people to grab. The faster we can push tasks through the bottleneck, the faster the whole system will go, so we don't want team members waiting around for valuable work to do. To avoid that problem, we create a "Publish Ready" buffer column (see Figure 25), which should never be empty. Whoever gets things ready to publish

FIGURE 25

Kanban Board + Buffer

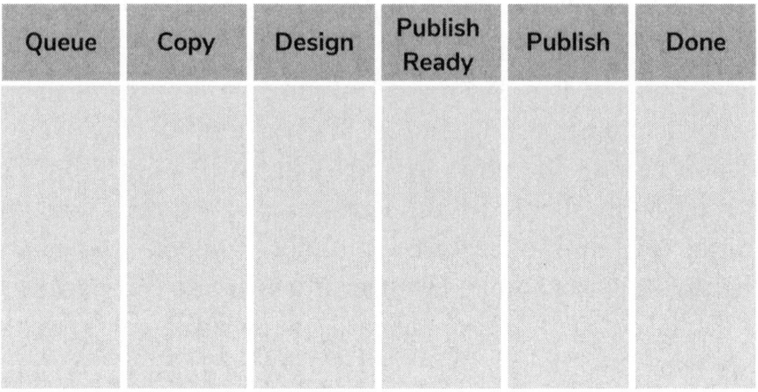

Queue	Copy	Design	Publish Ready	Publish	Done

Rimarketing Framework® AgileSherpas.

will ensure that something valuable always sits in that buffer column, waiting for the publishing folks.

Another practice that can be useful for teams who often find themselves waiting on other groups is including a "Pen" (short for holding pen) column on the workflow board. As discussed, WIP limits keep work flowing across the board, but if an item is out for review with another team, we don't want it occupying our WIP limit and slowing down our flow. We can't actively work on it, but if it hangs out in an active column, we are unable to start new assignments once we've hit our WIP limit. And we absolutely don't want to artificially inflate our WIP limit to accommodate this out-of-team work, because that will slow the entire system by increasing the number of items in progress. To remedy this situation, whenever a task leaves the execution team's control, we place it in the pen (see Figure 26).

The great thing about the pen is that the team can still see the task; it doesn't disappear from the board entirely. This delivers on the Rimarketing principle of radical transparency by showing us how much work we're waiting on others to complete. It also keeps the team informed about the volume of work that may come back to them. They won't be shocked when outside groups return tasks that need to be reincorporated into their workflow.

And speaking of returning to the workflow, we need one more column to make the pen work as well as it can. I call this the "Ready"

FIGURE 26

Kanban Board + PEN

Backlog	Creation	Editing	Done	Ready	PEN
	Initiative 1				
	Initiative 2				
	Initiative 3				

Rimarketing Framework® AgileSherpas.

column, but you can label it however you like. Its purpose is to show the team which items have left the pen and are ready to be worked on again. We can't just reinsert those tasks into an active column, because that could potentially violate the WIP limits. It also pushes work onto the team rather than allowing them to choose when they start on it, a surefire recipe for context switching.

Instead, items move from the pen to "Ready," showing that additional work is available to be taken back into the system. The team should have a policy for how to deal with these returning tasks. Usually that looks something like an agreement to check the Ready column whenever there's capacity, and to move work from there into an active column rather than take on something new from the queue.

It may be beneficial to track the amount of time a work item spends in the pen. This data point will help the team know which groups tend to take the longest to review work so they can plan accordingly.

Shared Practices: Queues

Whatever the board structure and WIP limits a team puts in place, they need a queue to fill it. In both flow and iteration states, the queue is the engine that powers a Rimarketing execution team. To function at the highest level, a queue should be well PACED:

Prioritized: There can be no side-by-side priorities in a Rimarketing queue. It must be ruthlessly prioritized, meaning there is one top priority, one second priority, and so on to the bottom. The execution team will always pull work from the top of the queue, so the most important tasks should be listed there. Team leads, through their prioritization activities, guide the team in doing the right work at the right time.

Accurate: The content of an item in the queue should accurately reflect the current understanding of that piece of work. If new information emerges after an experiment is run, the item needs an update. If we thought it would be due next month but the delivery requirements have changed, they need to be reflected on the card.

Current: The queue is not a "set it and forget it" tool. We don't refine it once a quarter; we update it constantly as new information comes to light. Whether a team lead chooses continuous queue refinement or recurring weekly meetings (see below for more on both of these), the queue should never be out of date or stale.

Educated: A major part of the team lead's job is to hunt down requirements and specifications for the work their team has been asked to do. Some of the essentials will come out during big-room planning, but others will need to be collected prior to work beginning. When we accept that we can't create a perfect plan up front, we also have to embrace the practice of continually adjusting projects in response to incoming data. All these activities should be reflected in the contents of the queue.

Detailed: Items look different depending on where they fall in the queue. The execution team will start working on things at the top very soon, which means those tasks need a much higher level of detail than tasks at the bottom. In fact, spending a lot of time chasing down information on low-priority items is a form of waste, because some of them might never make it to the top of the queue. Although the queue represents (nearly) all the work for an execution team during a quarter, we also welcome and plan for change. As things change, low-priority items may get pulled. They may also get delayed by emerging opportunities. In either case, we don't need to worry about collecting detailed requirements for tasks until they break into the top quarter of the queue.

Building and Refining Your Queue

If you're in a smaller organization where outlining the flow from executive leadership to teams at a great level of detail isn't necessary, you can generate a queue simply by listing all your upcoming marketing activities and ruthlessly prioritizing them. Remember, a queue includes not just big, strategic projects but also recurring business-as-usual work, at least as much as is relevant at this level.

This execution team backlog contains team-sized work that will take a couple of people a couple of weeks to complete, which means tiny tasks like "schedule social media sharing for the week" will be far too granular for the quarterly queue. So before they actually start work, the team will need to further break down items from the quarterly queue into their team queue. When in flow this will happen at whatever cadence the team chooses; when in iteration it happens at the beginning of each new iteration.

It's easy to get hung up on achieving exactly the right level of granularity for each stage of the queue, but not every work item has to be the same size. We place tasks into queues to gain visibility into all the work we *could* be doing, which then allows us to prioritize things against one another. Queues also reveal the true scope of work that a marketing team is tackling, allowing them to fend off external requests when necessary. We can achieve both these outcomes without precision in work item size.

Don't worry about getting things exactly right. Remember why you have a queue, and aim to create practices that help you complete the items it contains. As a starting point, listed below are some best practices to guide you. But be prepared to discuss your work items and their sizes in retrospective meetings and to make adjustments where needed.

Accepting Work into the Team's Queue

It would be amazing if marketing teams could sit down, plan their work for the next quarter, and then go off and do that work without any interruptions or dependencies. Unfortunately, we don't live in a fantasy world. Instead, we're beholden to all kinds of stakeholders and internal customers who have a say in what we do. This means we need a system that allows us to take in requests from outside the team in a way that accommodates everyone's needs (the team's and its stakeholders').

We need to strike a delicate balance here, because we don't want random hallway conversations dictating the work of the team and derailing our focus on strategic, planned tasks. On the other hand, we don't want to end up with massive briefs or requirements documents dictating every aspect of the team's activities. Consistency is the watchword for walking this tightrope.

If anyone—and I mean anyone, from the CMO to the newest hire—wants a Rimarketing team to do work for them, they should follow a designated process. That might be sending an email to a specific address, filling out an intake form, or creating an index card with agreed-on content. Whatever the system for accepting work, it needs to be the same across the board. It also needs to meet the team's definition of "ready": the criteria they've agreed on that determine whether they have all the information needed to start a task.

Each team will have its own, customized definition of ready. Yours might include:

- What audience segment or persona is being targeted?
- Is there a due date?
- Any preferred channels or tactics?
- What metrics should we track to determine success?
- Does this work align with our team's stated goals?

Anytime a request comes in that doesn't meet the criteria, the team lead should refuse to accept it into the team's queue. Otherwise an unclear item may end up at the top of the queue, and the team will lose valuable time chasing down its owner to answer the above questions (or many others). The team lead should spend a large part of his or her time ensuring that new items meet the definition of ready before they get prioritized.

Filling the Queue with the Right Work

Agile systems like Rimarketing deliver outstanding results for many reasons, but two of the most powerful are the combination of customer focus and speed. By providing customer value early and often, Agile teams create strong connections to the groups they serve. But to achieve this rapid delivery, each marketing team's queue must be filled with work that's designed to delight its customers in the short term while also meeting marketing's long-term objectives. For most execution teams, this means drastically changing the way work is designed.

Traditional marketing teams favor Big Bang campaigns, an approach that aligns with the waterfall style of project management. When doing work this way we spend a lot of time up front designing a perfect plan, and then proceed from stage to stage until the entire campaign is complete.

For marketing teams this may mean spending several weeks (or longer) on each stage, such as research and strategy, copywriting, design, editorial review, publication, amplification and promotion, etc. Not only do these kinds of projects take forever to complete; they carry huge risks. Because we receive no outside feedback until the entire campaign is finished, the whole thing could fail, and we won't know it until we've already devoted hundreds of hours and a huge chunk of our budget to getting it done.

When traditional teams who are used to running projects like this get introduced to Agile, they often mirror their old style of project management in the way they design work. They look at the stages of work and decide to spend a couple of iterations on research, then a couple on copy, a couple on design, and so forth. This approach is

FIGURE 27

Vertical vs. Horizontal Slices

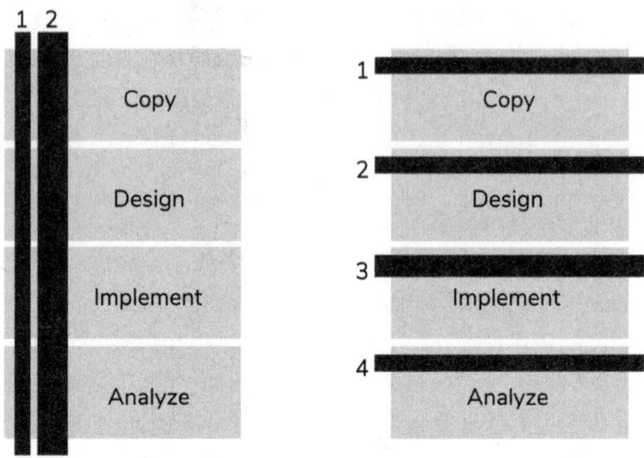

Rimarketing Framework® AgileSherpas.

known as horizontal slicing, and it doesn't accomplish tasks much faster than traditional waterfall project management. Instead, we want to get accustomed to slicing projects vertically, as illustrated in Figure 27.

Using this approach, we identify the minimum viable campaign or minimum viable project—in other words, the smallest number of things we could do and still meet the objectives for the work. We grab the highest-priority or highest-value tasks from each column and focus only on that until it's done. When finalized and delivered together, these items form a single useful increment that can be finished far sooner than if we completed *all* the work from one stage, then *all* the work from the next stage, and so on.

Estimating Effort (Not Hours) for Your Work

Once we've identified the subset of work that will form a minimum viable campaign, we need to go about the business of fulfilling it. But the obvious next question is how much can we truly accomplish in a set amount of time? To figure this out we estimate the amount of effort required to complete each item, then track how much work the team can tackle in a set amount of time. Once we have this body of data, we use the historical record to predict when certain items from the queue will be done.

Traditionally, only Scrum teams, those using recurring iterations, would estimate the effort for each item in their queue because they're concerned about accurately committing to completing a set amount of work in a sprint. Rimarketing teams, however, can make use of estimation whether they're in flow or iteration. As with most other components of the framework, we combine the effective parts of measurement from both traditions to create something unique for Agile marketing teams.

For those unfamiliar with estimation, it's worth reviewing some basic best practices here. If you've never estimated work before, take your time going through this section; many pitfalls lie in wait that can undermine your data's accuracy.

First of all, we estimate effort, not hours. Estimating hours is tempting because we can easily track and report on them, but it's precisely *because* they're so trackable that we avoid them. Hourly estimates are just too easy to manipulate and game. If I estimated for my editor that writing a chapter of this book would take me twelve hours, but through some spectacular inspiration it entailed only nine hours, chances are I'll still tell my editor it took twelve. I don't want her thinking that I slacked off, or that every single future chapter will only require nine hours. A stroke of luck allowed me to write that one chapter quickly, but the others might take much longer. I'm incentivized to be less than truthful about my hours.

But if we're estimating based on effort, I'm less prone to misrepresent the situation. My chapter required the same amount of effort, regardless of whether I exerted that effort over nine hours or twelve. Estimating based on effort helps capture more insight about the level of difficulty represented by certain kinds of work.

My preferred method of estimation is to use the Fibonacci sequence (don't worry, I'm not about to ask you to do advanced math). This is simply a series in which each third number is the sum of the two before it. It goes 1, 2, 3, 5, 8, 13, 21, and so on to infinity. The concept has emerged as the best way to estimate effort because the gaps between numbers increase as you go higher. If we use a regular, incremental series of numbers (1, 2, 3, 4, 5, 6, 7, 8, etc.), it becomes difficult to tell the difference between a four and a five. Even a six and an eight may be difficult to choose between. But when we jump several levels between options, it's easier to make a call. There's a big difference between an eight and the earlier numbers—it's four times harder than a two, and eight times harder than a one.

A creative director recently told me that her team "isn't into math," and was struggling to use the Fibonacci sequence for estimation. In cases such as these, a commonly used alternative is T-shirt sizes, such as small, medium, large, extra-large, and so on. The downside of this method is that we can't add things up to determine the average amount of work the team can complete in a set amount of time. If we did four smalls and an extra-large this week, but next week we're working on all mediums, how do we determine how many mediums we're likely to get done next week? With Fibonacci, however, we know that if we did four twos and a twenty-one this week, our throughput is twenty-nine. Then next week we can confidently predict that we'll complete four fives and one eight. The obvious workaround here is to equate each T-shirt size with a number and do the math after estimation is over, but in that case you might as well just estimate numerically.

Estimation remains a controversial topic in the Agile world, partially because humans are quite terrible at doing it accurately, and partially because it can take a lot of time. The former problem can't be entirely eradicated, but it can be mitigated as the team gains more experience in estimating. The latter problem, on the other hand, can be dealt with via some clever techniques that have evolved over the years. The first and most commonly used is known as planning poker. When used by an in-person team, the person running the estimation meeting reveals a work item and asks each team member to give an estimate of how much effort the task will require. Each member has a deck of cards (or sticky notes or whatever) with Fibonacci numbers on them, and they simultaneously show their choice. They do it at the same time, rather than one by one, so that no one gets anchored on a particular number. If I go first and vote that an item will require thirteen points of effort, everyone else is likely to be influenced by my choice. If everyone's choice is revealed simultaneously, however, each person can make their own judgement call. When there's general agreement about how hard something is (i.e., we all vote three or five), we don't need to discuss or debate it. The facilitator marks the level of effort with the most votes, and we move to the next item. Only when votes range wildly—that is, one person votes two and another votes thirteen—do we stop and discuss the work in greater detail. This approach lets us size a large amount of work quickly and (relatively) painlessly.

Planningpoker.com achieves a similar objective for virtual teams. Work items are loaded in advance and shown to team members via the website's interface; each person then votes on how much effort they believe is involved. No votes are shown until everyone has voted. At that point you can see if there's consensus about size or if discussion needs to happen. In both versions, in-person or virtual, teams who use planning poker can quickly estimate a high volume of work without debating every item individually.

Another option, known as affinity estimation, requires everyone to be in the same room. You create a sticky note for each potential work item, and then ask the entire team to move them around, ranking them in order from smallest to largest. They do this silently, again to avoid anchoring on a particularly vocal or persuasive team member. Each person can touch each sticky note as many times as they want. As with planning poker, the idea is to avoid talking about every single item. Those that nobody is worried about—the ones that get placed somewhere on the spectrum right away and are left alone—don't need to be discussed. Only those that keep getting moved around by two or more people require a debate.

After we have an agreed-on order, it's time to assign Fibonacci numbers. Each number in the sequence gets its own new sticky note, and then the team puts the sticky notes containing the work items into the category they believe best represents the item's level of effort. Tasks on the left or small end of the spectrum will go into the one, two, three, or five list, while those on the right are more likely to land in the eight, thirteen, or twenty-one lists.

As with the first step, the team proceeds in silence and can touch each sticky note as many times as needed. When agreement happens quickly, we assign the number and move on. When disagreement is clear, we can discuss the differing opinions and come to a compromise. I've seen a room of more than fifty people estimate over a hundred work items in half an hour this way. It's a remarkably efficient means of estimating without losing hours to the process.

As a final note about estimation, avoid the temptation to streamline the process by designating a team lead or other individual as the estimator. No single person knows everything about how work gets done. You'll obtain much more accurate data by allowing the team—the people responsible for accomplishing the tasks—to estimate the effort required.

There are a couple of exceptions to this rule. The first is when an item is very specialized—that is, only one person on the team will be doing it. We can rely on the subject-matter expert to estimate the effort required without taking it to the larger team. The second is when there's a potential discrepancy in effort depending on who's doing the work. For me to design and create a landing page from scratch would entail effort akin to running a marathon, but for my husband, who's an expert in development and user experience, to do the same would be a simple stroll around the block. Getting a variety of perspectives on estimation can help normalize these differences, but at times you may need to know who's responsible for doing the work before you can accurately determine how much effort will be involved.

Shared Practices: Rimarketing Meetings

Once the team has accepted and estimated work, it's time for them to focus on getting it done. Whether you have perfectly T-shaped people who could work on anything at any time or a team of highly specialized unicorns, you need meetings to keep things moving along. Because of its emphasis on enhancing focus and limiting work in progress, Rimarketing strives to eliminate as many meetings as possible. The ones that remain have clear objectives, and in fact they take the place of many traditional professional get-togethers. A few types of meeting happen only during the iteration phase of work, but several are common to both phases. We'll cover those four here.

Meeting 1: Daily Standup

Daily standup meetings are common across most (if not all) Agile frameworks, because they're one of the most powerful tools for removing impediments, increasing collaboration, and speeding up any sort of process. The problem is they're also easy to get wrong.

Traditional daily standup meetings happen, as you might imagine, every day. They last up to fifteen minutes, and every attendee should be standing to encourage brevity. Many Agile teams focus their standup conversations around three questions:

1. What did I do yesterday?
2. What do I plan to do today?
3. What impediments are in my way?

There's nothing wrong with this format per se, but if you follow it over and over again it can get a little stale. That's especially true for specialized marketing teams, where my work as a copywriter may or may not overlap with my teammate's work as a martech specialist. In those cases listening to my seemingly endless update about word count and edits and revisions may cause my martech colleague to check out. That means she doesn't hear me when I ask for help, or when I say something that could trigger an opportunity for us to work more closely together.

One of the things that causes these questions to break down over time is when a team comes to rely on them as a crutch. The daily standup meeting isn't about those three questions. It's about bringing a team together so that members can support one another as they complete great work in a short amount of time. It provides near-real-time visibility into progress and roadblocks so that both can be addressed rapidly and meaningfully. It reveals previously unknown ways for team members to work together.

If the three questions are serving your team and getting the results that standup meetings were made to deliver, then by all means use them as long as they're effective. But if standup has become a fifteen-minute daily death march, then it may be time to switch things up.

One option is to focus on the visualized workflow or kanban board rather than on individual updates from team members. A facilitator can use the board to discuss items that have changed status since yesterday (what got finished, what new work was started, what got blocked or unblocked). Individual team members chime in with questions, comments, and context as needed, but they refrain from detailing the minutiae of their day. The danger here is that detail gets omitted and opportunities for collaboration lost, but in specialized groups this may be the antidote to boring standups where nobody pays attention to anyone else's updates.

It's also vital to keep people on track during the standup. No meandering stories about pets allowed. Designate someone to run the meetings (it might be the team lead or rotating members), and keep participants focused on the conversation at hand. One team chose a code word to indicate that someone was getting off track, and anyone on the team was free to shout it whenever a team member lost focus during standup. Cries of "Squirrel!" often rang out from their area of the workspace each morning. That may be all you need to keep people on task.

Whatever strategy you devise, don't let standup deteriorate. Done well, standup can be the engine that drives continuous improvement across the team and its work. Neglected, it can be the first crack in a long descent into irrelevance for the Agile system the team has worked so hard to build.

Meetings across Multiple Teams: Scaled Daily Standup

In larger Rimarketing organizations, daily standup often needs to scale beyond a single team. If two or more execution teams are coordinating their efforts, if handoffs occur among teams, or if subject-matter experts need to be dynamically reallocated, then a scaled daily standup can be enormously helpful. Regardless of the driving factors, the meeting proceeds much the same way.

Ideally, the scaled daily standup happens right after the individual teams' standups, so any issues that were raised can be addressed as quickly as possible. If teams hold standup at 8:30 a.m., the scaled daily standup could start at 8:45 a.m. When there's a high degree of volatility or high demand for speedy completion in a group's workflow, the scaled meeting should happen every day. Some groups where things don't get done quite so quickly may be able to hold the scaled daily standup two or three times per week.

Once a time frame is settled on, team leads from each connected team get together and discuss the following:

- what their teams have accomplished since the last meeting
- plans for what will be done before the next meeting
- any problems that negatively affect their team's productivity
- possible impacts of their team's upcoming work on other teams
- feedback on how other teams' work might affect them

As with regular daily standup meetings, face-to-face meetings for the scaled daily standup are strongly preferred. Failing that, video can come in second, with phone a far distant third. Also like daily standups, a well-run scaled daily standup can unblock the flow of work and create previously unknown opportunities for collaboration across teams. You might be amazed to discover how much help becomes available when you allow for recurring moments of face-to-face interaction.

Meeting 2: Queue Refinement in Two Flavors

No matter its structure, the kind of work it does, its size, or its industry, every Rimarketing team shares the same engine: a queue. Analogous to the backlog you may have encountered in other Agile frameworks, the queue shows the team what tasks are most important for them to work on at any given time.

However, although the queue drives the team's work, maintaining the queue is *not* its job.

Part of the reason we distinguish between the What and How Cycles in Rimarketing is to free individual contributors from the mental load of both getting work done *and* determining whether the work they're doing aligns with larger priorities. If team members can focus exclusively on creating work of the highest possible quality, they're more likely to deliver outstanding results.

As discussed before, the team lead owns this part of the Rimarketing system: ensuring that the team can clearly identify and execute the highest-value work at all times. They can do this in a couple of ways: through continuous refinement or recurring meetings.

Option 1: Continuous Refinement

If your team lead can manage this approach, it's typically the most beneficial. As the name implies, the team lead constantly takes in new requests and prioritizes them against the work that's already in the queue. Some new items will make it right to the top of the list, while others will fall lower. Some will be rejected outright if they don't align with the execution team's focus or core KPIs.

As the team completes tasks, new items make their way to the top, and the team lead ensures that high-priority work is ready for the team to tackle. The team lead conducts fact-finding meetings, gathers requirements, liaises with stakeholders, and otherwise maintains the queue.

Team members aren't pulled into excessive numbers of meetings, nor do they spend hours each week navigating the political landscape and negotiating which tasks will be completed first. The idea here is not that the team is incapable of making such decisions, but rather that their time is more valuable when it's devoted to getting things done.

On the flip side, although we want to free the team from queue management whenever possible, that doesn't mean the team lead never consults team members. If the team lead doesn't fully understand a work item, can't decide how much effort a task might take, or is otherwise unsure how to proceed, they can always tap into the subject-matter expertise of individual team members. The important thing is to avoid overburdening the team.

In the continuous refinement mode, all of this happens in real time, meaning the queue is in a constant state of flux. Such an approach typically lends itself to the flow state, but it may be used during iteration as well.

Option 2: Regular Refinement Meetings

An alternative to ongoing refinement is to schedule recurring meetings to review, analyze, and reprioritize the queue. During iteration it's easy to set these up to coincide with the beginning of an iteration; during flow the team lead can create whatever cycle makes sense for the team's needs. Ultimately the schedule will depend on the team lead's efficiency (and how long it takes them to hunt people down), as well as the level of volatility in the work the team needs to complete. If stakeholders are habitually absent, or if priorities change often, queue refinement will probably need to happen every week or every other week to keep it current. If, on the other hand, gathering requirements goes smoothly and the team can predict what it's likely to be doing in three or four weeks, a monthly queue refinement session may be sufficient.

As with all aspects of Rimarketing, we strive for continuous improvement. Don't expect to nail the schedule the first time; be prepared to adjust it as you learn more about where the refinement bottlenecks are.

Queue Pro Tip: Balancing Urgency and Value

The most important factor in prioritizing the queue, regardless of how often that happens, is determining what work will deliver the most value for the customer (however you define "customer"). Work items with clearly defined and documented value should be completed first. Those with less certain outcomes fall down the list.

The exception to this guideline, of course, is when work comes with an immovable deadline. Sometimes deadlines are self-imposed, such as when you sponsor a conference. Booth components have a delivery deadline. Logos must be submitted on time. If you fail to book rooms on time, attendees won't have anywhere to stay. The list of tasks to accomplish is long, and none of its components are flexible. At other times, the deadlines aren't of your making, such as when sales suddenly books a demo with a massive potential client and you need to support them with custom collateral. In either case, urgency trumps value.

This is a reality of marketing work, and it should be reflected in the state of the queue. The team lead needs to be an expert in managing this balance, ensuring that work happens in the responsible window rather than the urgent window. In the responsible window the team remains in control of its workstream. They have deadlines, but they're able to incorporate them into high-value activities. In the urgent window they have to drop everything to tackle a task that's on fire. No matter how valuable another piece of work might be, it will be neglected while the deadline takes precedence.

Some Agile marketing teams have internalized a common rumor that Agile systems shouldn't take deadlines into account, but Rimarketing recognizes that this black-and-white mentality is simply unrealistic. The queue is designed to create visibility around both value and urgency, allowing the team lead to make intelligent tradeoffs that keep the team flowing smoothly while delivering on time.

Meeting 3: Stakeholder Interactions

Marketing is never an autonomous department. We're connected to nearly every other function inside an organization, which means we have to manage a lot of different stakeholder interactions. These touch points might be as simple as a salesperson requesting an updated one-sheet, or as complex as timing marketing campaigns with a major product launch. In both cases (and all the others in between), Rimarketing teams need to connect with other groups. This remains true whether the team is in iteration or flow.

A delicate balance must be struck here: we don't want to sidetrack the team with excessive meetings, but nor do we want problems to go unnoticed because we've lacked enough face time with partners. As if that balance alone weren't hard enough to manage, it's also likely that different stakeholders need different levels of interaction. And those levels may fluctuate from team to team.

Due to these complex factors, rather than create a prescriptive set of requirements for who a Rimarketing team should meet with and how often, in Figure 28 I provide a tool that each team can use to create its own preferred cadences.

The team labels the outer circle of the canvas with the *least frequent* interaction schedule they want to follow. In this example, it's labeled for quarterly interaction; for other teams it might be once a month. The label should equal the *longest* amount of time a team is comfortable going without talking to a stakeholder group.

The center circle contains the *most frequent* interaction schedule they'd like to have with a group. Usually that's daily (often at the daily

FIGURE 28

Stakeholder Interaction Canvas

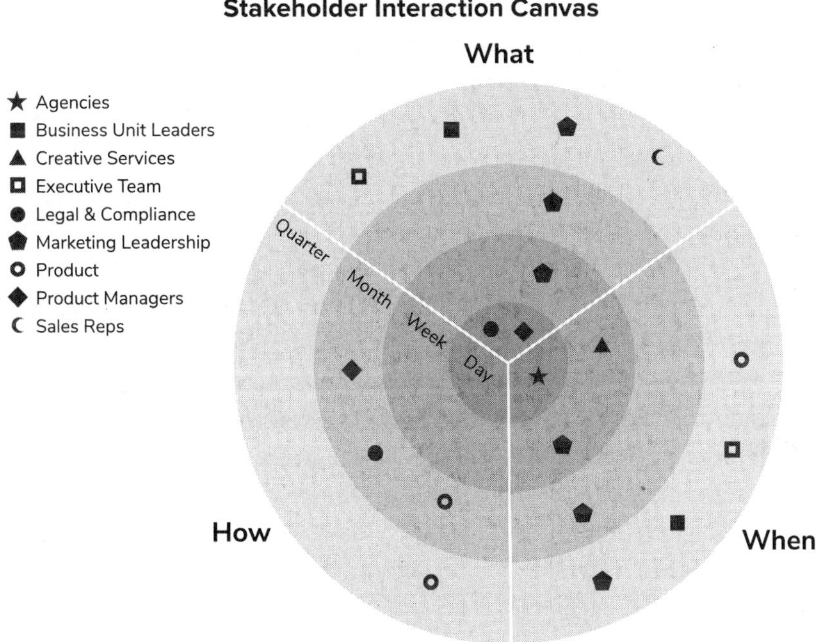

Rimarketing Framework® AgileSherpas.

standup meeting), but some teams may decide that's too often. Each circle in between gets labeled with a time period between the shortest and longest increments.

Next, it's time to decide which groups go where on the concentric circles. Each group has its own symbol for easy visibility; you could also use different colored sticky notes. In the completed version above, the team has chosen to connect with sales only once per quarter, but they'd like to touch base with someone from product management, the business units, and their agencies everyday.

For teams with relatively low levels of external interaction requirements, the canvas can act simply as a reminder of how often they need to be talking with different groups. However, for teams who spend a large amount of time managing stakeholder relationships, the canvas may serve as a visualization tool to reveal these high coordination costs. When a leader from another team swoops in and asks for a recurring weekly meeting to "check in with the team," the canvas quickly displays the impact such a cadence would have, and how many other meetings the team is already committed to.

In such cases, a team might create two versions of the stakeholder interaction canvas, one that represents the current state and one that shows the future state they want to move toward. The team lead can then work to change the frequencies to align with the team's preferences. Sometimes that means reducing the cadence (no need for daily chats with the business units after all), and at other times it means increasing it (if we could talk with legal more than once a month, we'd get more done).

Regardless of how you use the canvas, I recommend documenting each individual team's interactions on it. Per the Rimarketing principle of transparency, it helps to surface potential issues while also keeping the teams accountable to the groups they need to interface with.

Meeting 4: Retrospectives for Continuous Improvement

The core Agile meeting known as retrospective, or retro, allows the Rimarketing team to deliberately pause to reflect on their process. Too often we fly from project to project without taking time for inspection and adaptation; the retro is designed to counteract that tendency.

Retros are for the Rimarketing team only; no leadership or stakeholders should join. We restrict attendance to create an open environment for the team to have frank discussions about their current ways of working. There's nothing like having upper management in the room to shut down honest conversation.

If the queue is the engine of a great Rimarketing team, retros are the tune-ups that keep the system running smoothly. In the early days of a team's creation, it should meet every two weeks to talk about improvements in process. More mature teams may be able to hold retros slightly less frequently—say, three weeks apart. Going any longer risks degrading people's memories of what really happened at a process level. Details can fade, making the retros less effective if too much time passes between them.

Don't cut corners on retro meetings by allocating too little time for them. Plan for the team to spend at least a full hour in a room together. You may be tempted to "free up some time" by cutting retros short, but you need to create plenty of space for conversation to ramp up and keep flowing. The end of the day is a great time for a retro, especially if you bring snacks and turn it into a bit of a party.

However the discussion proceeds during the meeting itself, make sure your retros produce concrete action steps that the team will take to address the problems and opportunities that come up. There's nothing more disheartening than rehashing the same topics week after week after week because change hasn't occurred. If needed, create new items to include in the team's queue so the team lead can prioritize the team's chosen improvements alongside its other work. Select a scribe for each retro who'll capture the most salient discussion points, action items, and owners of those items to ensure that the meetings lead to action.

Finally, team leads should be prepared to guide the retro, especially when the team isn't yet familiar with the meeting or its purpose. Some common formats for kicking off a retro are to ask the team to think of events from the past two weeks and place them into predetermined categories. Sample categories include Stop/Start/Continue (what should the team stop doing, start doing, continue doing), Liked/Lacked/Learned/Longed For, and Mad/Sad/Glad. Allow individuals to brainstorm quietly for several minutes before opening the floor to discussion. (Introverted team members will be deeply thankful for this time.) Each team member creates a sticky note for each event or idea and places it in the appropriate category. Then the team lead can walk through the items, guiding the team through group discussion.

If a team lead isn't experienced in running this kind of meeting, I strongly recommend the book *Agile Retrospectives*, by Esther Derby and Diana Larsen, for a nearly endless source of ways to keep it fresh.

The Execution Team in Flow

Now that we've established a few best practices, we're ready to dive deeper into the Rimarketing execution team's default way of working: continuous flow. The easiest way to understand a team in flow is to follow one through its typical activities, so that's how this section is structured.

We'll begin at the start of a new quarter, when the execution team has just returned from its big-room planning session. Following that meeting they should have a prioritized project-level queue, but it doesn't yet incorporate their business-as-usual work. Remember that items in the BRP-generated queue can be completed by a couple of people in a couple of weeks. The team will need to break them down into smaller parts and add their BAU items. Execution teams can determine how often they want to do this activity when in flow, and their decision will likely depend on the volatility of their environment and the speed with which they accomplish their work.

Some advanced teams can do just-in-time (JIT) planning. That is, whenever the team gets ready to start a new, large project, they hold a quick meeting to divvy up the tasks. Less mature teams, or those that lack experience with the work they'll be doing, will want to hold regular planning meetings in which they task out items in the queue that they plan to start over the next few days. They might even break things out for weeks in advance, though this is the exception rather than the rule. Each execution team employs slightly different timing for queue refinement and planning while in flow, so be prepared to experiment. Start with planning every week and see how that feels, then discuss it during a retro and adjust as needed.

Now is also the time when each member of the team incorporates into the queue any BAU work they're responsible for, and the team lead helps to ensure that it's appropriately prioritized against project work. To be frank, this aspect of planning can be time consuming and a bit tedious at first, but it's an important part of the Rimarketing principle of radical transparency. Taking the time to get everyone's work out in the open can reveal previously unseen time-sucking black holes, which the team lead can help to mitigate or remove.

As a bonus, once all the work is visible, it becomes far easier to show stakeholders and marketing leadership how busy people really are. As requests come in, you can ask that they be prioritized against the full scope of a person or team's commitments rather than just the project work.

A Typical Day in Flow

Once the team has a quarterly queue that's been broken into manageable pieces, each person will take a look at it. They'll select the highest-priority item they're able to work on, attach their name to it, and get started. Early in the day—let's say at 9:00 a.m.—the team will have its daily standup meeting.

Since the team has just started a new round of work, members won't have anything to report about the prior day's activities, but they will share their plans for the upcoming twenty-four hours. Any predicted dependencies or handoffs among team members may also be discussed, for example, "I'm doing the copy for this landing page today, and I'll have something to work with design on tomorrow." This micro-cycle continues each day while the team is in flow. Team members pull work when they have capacity, work on it independently or with other team members until it's done, and then move to the next item in the queue.

If you have a team of specialists, tasks may be completed mostly independently, with occasional moments of collaboration. On a more cross-functional team, the balance will tip the other way, with very little solo work and more shared effort. Either way, daily standup meetings keep everyone in sync, ensure timely collaboration, and help people address impediments that come up. Assignments may get blocked, which should be noted in a visible way, but even when that happens plenty of activities should still be available for all team members. WIP limits should ensure a steady flow of work through the team from day to day.

In a larger Rimarketing system—that is, one with three or more execution teams—the team leads will also meet daily with the strategy group. This meeting happens after the scaled daily standup (introduced earlier in the chapter, and which takes place following each execution team's standup). The team leads convey to the strategy group pertinent information from their teams' standups, escalate any major hurdles the team is encountering, and coordinate efforts with other team leads.

Note that team members are *pulling* work when they're available, rather than being assigned work by the team lead. Additionally, if items in the queue need to be broken into smaller chunks and owned by different team members, it's up to the team to take care of that. They may need a weekly planning meeting to do so, which is typically a good Monday morning activity. It should be a relatively quick meeting (an hour should cover a week's worth of work) that allows everyone on the team to pull items from the queue without wasting time investigating what their part of a larger project needs to be.

Incorporating Subject-Matter Experts and Reviews

Wrinkles are likely to crop up that will need to be addressed within this cycle of continuous flow. One such wrinkle is the incorporation of subject-matter experts (SMEs). Most marketing departments aren't perfectly resource balanced, meaning they have a handful of people that many teams need access to but whom nobody needs all the time. These individuals' roles vary widely from one organization to another, but common SMEs include search-engine optimization (SEO) specialists, content strategists, and editorial reviewers. Regardless of who your SMEs are, they need to be incorporated into the Rimarketing flow.

The weekly planning session described above is crucial to ensuring that SMEs are available when the team requires them. Likewise, if they're in high demand across multiple execution teams, the scaled daily standup is there to allow team leads to negotiate SME time while minimizing waste and waiting and avoiding overburdening the SMEs.

As work proceeds within flow, the execution team will want to periodically obtain input and feedback from the strategy group through review meetings. Depending on the project, some execution teams will require such meetings more frequently than others. For example, an execution team exploring an emerging channel, targeting a new persona, or otherwise working on something new may want to check in with their strategy group every week. An execution team that is supporting events may have their process dialed in and need far less input. They may request a strategy group meeting every three weeks. Each execution team will establish their own meeting cadence, and the strategy group should honor the request unless they have a good reason to question it. In that case, their concern can be aired at a retrospective meeting or communicated to the team lead, who can discuss it with the execution team. Ultimately, aim to establish sufficient oversight around strategic alignment, brand compliance, and other long-term interests without babysitting the execution team or slowing down their ability to get work done.

Improving Flow by Eliminating Meetings

Strategy group reviews, in conjunction with daily standups and the visualization of work via a kanban board, should replace all status meetings. No execution team member should be pulled out of their daily work to provide an update on how that work is proceeding. If the board fails to communicate status with enough specificity, a request for further detail should go through the team lead. Having just attended a standup meeting, the lead should be able to provide the necessary insight. Excessive meetings are some of the biggest wasters of time in modern knowledge work, and Rimarketing strives to eliminate them whenever possible. All meetings have a clearly defined purpose and happen as infrequently as is feasible.

Sometime in the last decade or so we began to equate our level of importance with the number of meeting invitations on our calendars. Many teams I coach tell me they have literally an hour per day to actually work; they spend the rest of their time in meetings. This isn't acceptable, productive, or pleasant, and Rimarketing is designed to clear calendars so that real work can happen.

If you're currently operating in a culture that equates busyness with importance, you may have some work ahead of you to disentangle activity from value creation. Accomplishing tasks that serve our customers and audiences (and supporting our teammates in doing the same) makes us productive team members. Sitting in hour after hour of meetings does not.

One meeting that *does* still need to happen is queue refinement. As the team proceeds, their queue needs to stay updated so that they

(1) are working on the highest-priority items at all times, and (2) have all the information they need to execute those tasks. The team lead is responsible for ensuring that the execution team's queue is current. Some team leads know enough about the organization and the execution team to refine the queue independently. They'll do it on their own time. Other team leads lack specialized knowledge about everything an execution team works on, which is very common in teams that tackle a wide variety of assignments. In this case, the team lead needs help from the team to keep the queue current.

When the team lead needs input from the team to refine the queue, they have a couple of options:

1. **Weekly refinement:** Set aside a particular window of time each week to refine the queue, usually two to four hours, depending on the volume and complexity of work in play. During that period, execution team members know to make themselves available to the team lead to answer questions. The team lead may need to call on individuals either for a quick consultation or for longer. Either way, members of the execution team are not required to sit in an hours-long meeting when their input may be required for only ten minutes.
2. **Just-in-time refinement:** Refine the queue in a JIT fashion, conferring with execution team members as needed. In this scenario, the team lead is refining the backlog almost constantly. Whenever a new request comes in, they compare it to the existing contents of the queue and place it where it belongs. As work moves closer to the top, the team lead sets up meetings and gathers requirements. To do all of this in an organic, real-time way, the team lead will likely need to tap into the expertise of various team members. The daily standup should offer an ideal time to let team members know when they'll be called on to contribute so they can adjust their plans accordingly. As with weekly refinement, some people will need to spend an hour or more helping the team lead, while others may need to answer only a few quick questions.

TABLE 4

Rimarketing Activities Handled in Flow

Rimarketing Practice	How It's Handled in Flow
Queue refinement	Team lead keeps the queue up to date at all times, via either continuous (JIT) refinement or scheduled recurring sessions.
Daily standup	Execution team meets every day for fifteen minutes to discuss progress.
SME allocation	General allocation determined at big-room planning. Dynamic adjustments made throughout the quarter at scaled daily standups.
Stakeholder feedback	Execution teams request feedback as needed. Recurring sessions are mapped on the stakeholder interaction canvas. Ad hoc sessions may take place but should happen as rarely as possible.
Interaction with strategy group	Each execution team sets its own cadence for connecting with the strategy group. Team leads meet with one another and the strategy group in the scaled daily standup.
Task distribution and planning	May occur on a JIT basis or on a regular schedule, depending on the execution team's preference.

Whatever system a team lead uses, the important thing is for individual contributors to provide their unique insight when it's required without being overburdened with unnecessary meetings.

Table 4 summarizes the Rimarketing activities typical of the flow state.

Specialists versus Cross-Functional People

As you can imagine, flow can be easily interrupted when the execution team is made up of specialists. When only one person can perform a particular function, the process gets disrupted when that person is out of the office, too busy to help, or otherwise unavailable. Things proceed more smoothly with cross-functional team members (the T-shaped people we met in Part Two).

Many marketers were hired for their specializations, and they may resist the push to generalize their skill set, but a team can go faster if it consists of individuals who possess abilities the team needs. Remember that not everyone needs to be an expert in everything; basic knowledge that allows someone to lend a hand is often enough to keep tasks moving forward.

The Execution Team in Iteration

From time to time, an execution team may choose to pause its flow and move into a more iterative style of working.[1] While in the flow state, team members choose high-priority items from the queue, complete them, and move on to the next ones. Their queue is regularly refined and replenished by the team lead, and they conduct retrospectives to inspect and adapt their process. As the term implies, a team in flow delivers work in a continuous, uninterrupted flow. They are prepared to take in work at any time, reprioritize often, and generally go with the flow of their professional obligations. Situations may arise, however, when the team no longer wants to accept this constant change, when flexibility needs to give way to focus. At that point the team moves into a phase of iteration.

Iteration is a distinct way of executing work that begins with a planning meeting, during which the team determines:

1. the length of their upcoming iterations
2. what work needs to be accomplished before the iterative stage can be considered complete
3. how many iterations are required to complete the work (an estimate that the team is free to adjust as they go)

---

1. Scrum practitioners will notice similarities to the Scrum framework in this description. Although based on Scrum, these iterations are designed to be a subset of the team's activities, rather than continuously recurring, back-to-back sprints. I believe this distinction separates the concept from traditional Scrum, making the usual Scrum naming conventions confusing rather than helpful for our purposes. I also want to help marketing teams think about their agility as a personalized, customized approach and avoid getting caught up in existing terminologies or best practices.

The iteration phase consists of a series of consecutive iterations, during which the team focuses on a small amount of work. This is a different method of limiting work in progress, one that forces the team to narrow its scope for a brief time. The iteration plan outlines what the team needs to accomplish, and they do their best to stick to it until the iteration concludes.

Iterations work best when they're short (between one and three weeks), because even when the execution team locks down to focus on set tasks, they don't want to prevent themselves from being able to respond to changes for too long. A six-week iteration means that all external requests and reprioritizations will be put on hold for that time, which can feel like an eternity if you're a sales team that needs marketing's help for a project.

If you're unsure what the length of your iteration should be, start with two weeks. You'll get a feel for whether you should adjust up, down, or not at all for future iteration phases. But whatever length you choose, it should stay consistent throughout the iteration phase. Keeping the length the same allows the team to accurately estimate how much they'll be able to accomplish from iteration to iteration; if the length changes, the team won't be comparing apples to apples.

As mentioned, the iteration phase begins with the first planning session. The team gathers to decide what they'll commit to completing during their first iteration. They examine their queue, paying particular attention to whatever project, campaign, hurdle, or other obligation sparked their entrance into iteration, and decide how much they can and must accomplish in the next couple of weeks.

Whatever you do, don't skimp on planning time! The team needs to commit with accuracy and confidence to their plan, which means they need ample time to hash out details and dependencies before jumping into the work. A good rule of thumb is to allow one hour for every week of the iteration; thus, a two-week iteration will take about two hours to plan.

By the end of the planning session, the execution team will have built an iteration queue, which will serve as their guide for what needs to get done during the iteration. Their larger team queue still exists, and it can continue to accept work and be rearranged during the iteration. The iteration queue, however, is static once the execution team commits to it. The purpose of entering iteration is to create the conditions for effective, focused delivery, which means the iteration queue should be locked down. The team lead can accept new requests in the main queue, but only unavoidable emergencies should disturb the execution team in iteration.

Table 5 summarizes how a team's activities are handled during iteration. Take a moment to compare it with Table 4, "Rimarketing Activities Handled in Flow."

If the execution team will be moving through two or more consecutive iterations, it can be helpful to pause between them for a retrospective meeting. Like the retros that take place during flow, this session lets them discuss the outcomes from earlier iterations, making adjustments as needed to improve their performance going forward.

TABLE 5

Rimarketing Activities Handled in Iteration

Rimarketing Practice	How It's Handled in Iteration
Queue refinement	The execution team creates an iteration queue, which is set and no longer refined. The team lead may continue to refine the larger team queue while the iteration proceeds.
Daily standup	Same as in flow. Execution team meets every day for fifteen minutes to discuss progress.
SME allocation	General allocation timing determined at big-room planning. SMEs may join an execution team for one or more iterations, depending on the work being done. Ideally an SME fully commits to a team that's entered an iteration phase.
Stakeholder feedback	Collected at the end of each iteration through iteration review, as well as at the conclusion of the iteration phase.
Interaction with strategy group	Ideally confined to iteration review. The execution team may request ad hoc input as needed.
Task distribution and planning	Occurs during iteration planning.

The stakeholder reviews discussed earlier should almost always pause during an iteration. Setting this limit allows for greater focus within the iteration by eliminating a meeting. To continue aligning with larger strategic goals and obtain timely feedback, the execution team conducts a more formal review session after each iteration. They also conduct an overall review when all their iterations (and therefore the project they needed to focus on) conclude.

Analogous to a software demo, the iteration review provides an opportunity for the execution team to reveal the output of their focused work. There's no need to spend hours creating beautiful slides for this meeting; its contents should consist of whatever the execution team produced during the iteration. Stakeholders, internal partners, executives, and anyone who may need to use the execution team's output should attend. The review is the time to learn everything about what the execution team committed itself to executing, making it a very important meeting.

Differences between Flow and Iteration

As you can imagine, many differences exist between an execution team in flow and one in iteration. Rimarketing envisions flow as the primary state, so it's where you'd expect to find the execution team most of the time. While in this state the team flexes and adapts on a daily basis. Their queue is refined often as new requests come in and are prioritized. Team members grab high-priority items, work on them to completion, and then proceed to new tasks. Low WIP limits keep work flowing smoothly. Stakeholders and marketing leaders both have regular touchpoints with the team.

In iteration, the vibe of the execution team changes. Something has come up to demand their focus, and in some respects they close ranks, restricting the access of outsiders. They commit their time and energy to a small subset of the tasks in their queue, and they work diligently together to get them done. Other items take a backseat. They continue holding their regular retrospectives and daily standups, but they may suspend sessions with the strategy group and external stakeholders.

Does Everyone on the Team Have to Iterate Simultaneously?

When I first came up with the flow/iteration/flow cycle for Agile marketing teams, I envisioned everyone on the team moving through the phases in sync. The entire execution team would flow together until a meaningful reason to iterate appeared. They would complete a series of iterations as a unit, and then they would return to flow as one. But the first several teams to whom I presented the concepts asked me the same question: could some of the team lock themselves into iteration while the rest of the team continued in flow?

My initial reaction was no; the entire execution team should be working together. If they need to split their methods significantly, are they even cut out to be a persistent team?

However, in the interest of continuous improvement and validated learning, I want to present the possibility for this variation to the broader Agile marketing community. As of this writing I haven't coached a team that has split itself between flow and iteration, but I don't want to preemptively shut this avenue down.

Check MasteringMarketingAgility.com for regular updates on this front.

The iteration phase, because it's infrequent and occurs only in times of serious focused effort, should be respected by those outside the execution team. In its usual state the execution team takes incoming requests freely, incorporating them into its queue and flowing rapidly through assignments. Iteration happens rarely, and outsiders need to allow the team to move into it and remain there when the team believes it will be the best way to complete important work.

The events that trigger a move from flow to iteration are many and varied. In essence, the execution team needs to enter iteration when they encounter work in their queue that is:

- **Unusually large:** Running a user conference, supporting a product launch, or drafting a new content strategy would all qualify as substantially larger than the work marketing teams typically do. Each of them might warrant a series of iterations to create the right conditions for focused execution. The caveat here is that even when iterating on large work items, the team needs to break the work down into smaller, manageable pieces that can be completed rapidly. Otherwise the team risks slipping into old waterfall styles of project management that won't support the rapid delivery that modern marketing demands.

- **Complex:** Almost every execution team has items in its queue that are more complicated than others. These complex tasks may require a lot of agency support, involve multiple channels, or demand coordination with other execution teams. Whatever their exact makeup, complex assignments can be easier to deal with in iteration than in flow.
- **Unknown:** When I help marketing teams learn about iterative work, I use a simulation that involves folding origami fish. There's almost never anyone in class who's an expert in origami; iterations are therefore the best way to handle this unfamiliar task. You probably won't do origami as part of your marketing efforts, but if you encounter an unknown it may be time to circle the wagons and iterate until your execution team figures it out.
- **Urgent:** This one is the most obvious. You may only need iteration to handle an urgent work item if it also meets one of the other criteria on this list. A task that's merely urgent could quite possibly be tackled by an execution team in flow. The team lead moves it to the top of the queue, where someone grabs it quickly and works on it to completion. A team might even break its usual WIP limits to address the urgent item right away rather than waiting for capacity to open up in the system. Whatever the tactics used, many execution teams can handle work that's urgent without breaking into iteration. If the assignment is both urgent *and* complex, unknown, or large, then iteration is the way to go.

You'll notice that the first three criteria have something in common: if handled within flow, work that meets these conditions has the potential to take a long time. In traditional project management, new, complex, large projects are notorious for dragging on. They miss deadlines, go over budget, and otherwise fail. A good execution team should deliver early and often in flow, but work that falls into the above categories calls for deliberate focus to save it from the typical fate.

Measuring Rimarketing in Flow and Iteration

Regardless of what state an execution team is in, it needs to be aware of how it's performing. That means tracking effectiveness at two different levels: process and marketing. Process-level metrics tell us if Rimarketing is doing its job—in other words, if the team is getting more done in less time. Marketing-level metrics measure the same things we've always measured (or at least should have always measured). They indicate whether the execution team's activities provide the expected outcomes.

Measuring Process

There are two primary methods of measuring process: cycle time and throughput. An execution team can get away with tracking only one, but keeping an eye on both improves predictability for upcoming work.

Cycle time is simply how long it takes a work item (something from the queue) to make it through the execution team's entire workflow. Said another way, how much time passes between when the team starts on a task and when they finish it? Most digital tools, both the Agile and the traditional project management variety, should have this capability built in.

If an execution team is using good old-fashioned sticky notes, they jot down the date when they started an assignment and then the date they finished it. Their cycle time is the difference between the dates. So if a team started a task on Tuesday and finished it on Friday of the following week, they had a cycle time of nine days (we don't count weekends, because after all we're supposed to be working at a sustainable pace). See Table 6 for other examples.

TABLE 6
Cycle Time Measurement

Date Started	Date Finished	Cycle Time
Monday morning	Wednesday afternoon	3 days
Monday morning	Monday afternoon	1 day
Monday morning	Next Friday morning	10 days

I like measuring cycle time because it smooths out some of the variability that comes with marketing work. Certain small items, like writing a weekly blog post, never take long. Others, like drafting a new content strategy, take far longer. Cycle time lets us embrace these different scales without getting caught up in making every item in the queue the exact same size. After tracking cycle time for several weeks, we can reach a meaningful average that allows us to predict delivery time before we start tasks.

Measuring cycle time helps control for the variations in work, but you can also track the cycle times of different types of work if that data point is useful for your execution teams or strategy group. You might track content-creation tasks in one table and strategic-planning work in another. Then you can compare different types of assignments with more specificity. You *could* measure an infinite number of things; instead, decide which ones will deliver the insight you need and track only those. If knowing the different cycle times for different kinds of work might be useful, then by all means measure each one. If you can't imagine what you'd do with that data, or if the team doesn't work on a wide variety of tasks, focus on overall cycle time.

The second process-level metric is throughput, or the number of items an execution team completes in a set period of time (usually a week). Like cycle time, throughput is agnostic about the type of work. It doesn't care if the team finished five blog posts and two emails, or three social media campaigns, three landing pages, and one ebook. In both cases the throughput is seven.

This data point is particularly powerful when predicting future delivery for tasks that are positioned lower in the execution team's queue. If a team finishes about eight work items per week, and a stakeholder asks the team lead about an item that's twenty-fourth in the queue, the team lead can predict that the execution team is likely to complete that item within three weeks (assuming, of course, that nothing happens to disrupt the order of the queue).

To track throughput, every Friday afternoon the team lead tallies up all the items the execution team completed that week. If the team uses a physical board, doing this simply involves counting what's in the "Done" column. A digital tool will quickly sort all the items marked as complete in the past week.

Cycle time and throughput work in both the flow and iteration phases, so you don't have to change the way you're tracking the execution team if they move into an iteration.

A third—and optional—process-level metric is rounds of revision. It's most useful for execution teams that depend on external reviews with creative directors, legal, or other groups that are likely to request multiple rounds of changes to the team's work. This back-and-forth may eat up days, or even weeks, so reducing the number of handoffs can be valuable. If an execution team has gotten stuck in endless rounds of review, you may want to keep track of how often tasks usually get revised. Fewer revisions indicate a more collaborative process, and they certainly indicate gains in process efficiency.

Measuring Marketing Outcomes

As you gain a better understanding of how Rimarketing helps an execution team accomplish more in less time, keep an eye on whether they're doing the right work at the right time. I can't give you a blueprint for this part, because every marketing department evaluates success in a different way. But whether your primary success metric is a gain in marketing qualified leads (MQLs), email subscribers, or paid conversions, you want to know if you're achieving more of it following a Rimarketing rollout.

As mentioned earlier, marketing-level metrics may vary. Even so, you should have in place a few overarching metrics that all execution teams can roll up to. A software-as-a-service (SaaS) company, for instance, might have a yearly goal to reduce churn in its subscriber base. Each execution team might work on smaller metrics, but they should also be able to show how their overall efforts contribute to the larger marketing objective of reducing churn.

As you can imagine, all these metrics bear the biggest impact when viewed from a before-and-after perspective. Ideally, an execution team will take a look at its past performance before undertaking Rimarketing, and then compare it to outcomes following the transformation. If new execution teams were created as part of the Rimarketing rollout, obtain a departmental average for both process- and marketing-level data points. This is the best way to determine the impact of your Rimarketing efforts.

If, for instance, you know that most marketing projects currently take three months to deliver, and by following a Rimarketing pilot a new execution team delivers a similar assignment in just two weeks, you can point to a 6x improvement in delivery time (a common level of improvement for Agile teams). During their pilot efforts, the Agile marketers at CA Technologies reduced their delivery time from two months to two weeks. If a project-based team of eight people typically completes three items per week (I know I'm being generous), but a Rimarketing execution team cranks out twenty-four tasks each week, they've achieved a 700 percent improvement in output.

Even if we don't have the capability to take a before-and-after snapshot of marketing outcomes, we can extrapolate the impact of the easily measured process metrics. If campaigns usually deliver a hundred MQLs, and now we can deliver twenty-six campaigns per year (one every two weeks) rather than four per year (one every three months), we've increased from four hundred MQLs per year to twenty-six hundred. If a typical content item provides ten new email subscribers per week, and we can now complete six per week when we were doing three, we've doubled our rate of subscriber generation.

Of course, the rapid feedback loops of Rimarketing ensure that even marketing outcomes improve. We have far more opportunities to iterate on our efforts when the execution teams, strategy groups, and leadership team regularly connect. Campaigns and projects come up for iteration more frequently, and each adjustment increases the potential to improve marketing's impact. Consider the usual marketing cadence. We race around to finish a campaign, hustle it out the door right at the deadline, and immediately turn our attention to the next thing looming on the horizon. We're too busy rushing forward to review our past work. In the process we miss crucial opportunities for learning and improvement.

But in a Rimarketing environment, pauses are mandatory. We have regularly scheduled check-ins with our strategy group, who should provide their expertise on campaign metrics and suggest ideas for improvement. Packs connect individual teams every few weeks, so the lessons from one team's successful (or unsuccessful) campaign can be applied to future efforts.

For instance, the CA team from earlier tripled their win rate for marketing-sourced opportunities and saw a 20 percent increase in their leads pipeline without increasing their budget.

This is where the Agile magic really starts to show itself. More work, less time, bigger impact. That's the power of agility in action.

Where Do Subject-Matter Experts Fit In?

Before we close the section on practices, we need to talk in more detail about subject-matter experts. These folks are often the thorn in the side of marketing organizations looking to reorganize in a more cross-functional, customer-centric way. The problem comes down to this: if we need to build four execution teams based on stages of the customer journey but we have only one SEO expert, where does that person sit?

Usually there's more than one SME, and the tendency is to put each of them on all the teams so they can provide insight to everyone. But the moment this happens we've put our rapid feedback loops and the focus of individual contributors in jeopardy, because we've quadrupled (at least) the inputs for all the SMEs. If the SEO expert is on four teams, she's got four daily standups to attend. Four boards to monitor. Four queues to prioritize against one another. In other words, she's in for a huge amount of context-switching and decision-making overhead. She'll spend far too much time navigating the process and not nearly enough adding value with her expertise.

This inequitable resourcing can be handled in two ways. The first is more common in small to mid-sized marketing organizations with just a few SMEs to manage. In this case the SMEs don't belong to any single execution team. They're part of the strategy group only, and the members of the strategy group determine which team the SMEs assist and when. As you recall, the strategy group has a scaled daily standup with representatives of the execution teams that it serves. This is when the strategy group hears the needs of the execution teams and dynamically allocates the SMEs where they can deliver the most value.

It may become clear during quarterly big-room planning that a particular execution team will need to borrow an SME for an extended period of time. In that case, one outcome of BRP might be to send an SME to that team for the quarter, or however long it takes to complete the project they're advising on.

The second option for handling SMEs works best when you have enough of them (at least four) to form an execution team. In this case they make up their own distinct team, complete with a team lead, who accepts requests into a queue and prioritizes them for execution by team members. When necessary, members of the SME team may join meetings with other execution teams, but often they focus on a flow-centric process that allows them to complete requests from other teams in a rapid, just-in-time fashion.

What Happens when Your Partners Aren't Agile (Yet)?

One of the questions I hear all the time from new execution teams is how they can commit to improving their own practices when their partners aren't ready to change. Sometimes that means internal groups (legal, human resources, maybe even product development); at other times it means external partners, usually agencies.

Here's the thing: Agile development teams have been the lone pockets of agility in many, many organizations for about two decades.

They realized that if they were going to have any chance at breaking free of the horrible cycle they were in, they had to make radical changes, and they couldn't wait for everyone else to get on board.

Marketers, we're in the same boat now. You can bemoan the sluggishness of business units, stakeholders, and vendors and use their pace as an excuse to avoid change. Or you can commit to doing everything within your power to optimize the things you *can* control.

Marketing is powerful. Our profession touches customers throughout their engagement with a brand, and we have a unique opportunity to influence the adoption of agility across the organization. Not everyone we encounter will move with our nimble grace. They won't be as responsive to customer needs. But that's no excuse for us to turn away from the potential offered by marketing agility.

Take the steps outlined in these pages, and document whatever drag non-Agile partners have on your effectiveness. Once you've exhausted avenues for improvement inside your own system (which is likely to take quite a while), you can turn your attention to the external pieces and begin to work through the bottlenecks. Don't worry—you'll have plenty to do in the meantime.

PART 5

TRANSFORMATION
The Path from Here to There

> In terms of technique, shu is a time for technical mastery in which you pass through the bulk of the art's technical repertoire; ha offers an opportunity to research and apply those techniques; ri is the completion of something that is your own.
>
> KAZUO CHIBA, AS REPORTED IN THE *AIKIDO JOURNAL*

WELL, HERE WE ARE. You've got all the pieces needed to transform your marketing operations into a lean, mean, Agile execution machine. You're ready to create a shared foundation of principles around which you can organize teams and strategy. You've got a robust list of practices and change-proof processes to keep both your long-term perspective and your daily activities on track. So . . . what now? Where do you start?

If you have a larger department—forty people or more—you need to begin with a pilot group or two. We'll get to those in a moment. Smaller marketing organizations could potentially flip the switch and change everyone's processes overnight. I've seen a forty-person department go through a two-day training together, reach a consensus that they were ready for drastic change, and make the complete transition in a week. They built four new teams based on parts of the funnel (top, middle, bottom, and retention) and committed to new Agile practices within the teams.

They hold the record for the fastest-changing group I've ever worked with, and it was amazing to see (shout out to you guys if you're reading this—you know who you are). That pace isn't ideal for everyone, but if you've got a smallish group, you have the potential to make tremendous strides in a short time. You need two things:

1. **Consensus:** Building consensus is key to making this kind of change work. In the overnight switch that I talked about, the entire department knew they needed to do something different, and they could see the power of Agile marketing to meet that need. Some objections were voiced, but we took the time to talk through them and establish plans for mitigating the risks raised. It was this agreement to take action that allowed for rapid change.

2. **Shared understanding:** This is a prerequisite for consensus, because having different interpretations of agility within a group will set the stage for problems. I can't overstate the value of getting everyone together in the same room for education (even if that room is virtual). Teams who learn together refer back to the lessons they gained and use them as a foundation on which to build true agility. For instance, we do a simple demonstration of agility using pennies, and clients continually refer to that activity when misunderstandings arise about things like batch sizes and sustainable pace. Without having gone through the exercise together, they would lack that point of reference. Compared to teams who send one "leader" to training and then have them try to relay the knowledge, groups with a true shared understanding progress faster and suffer fewer setbacks.

The Perils of Pilots (and How to Avoid Them)

If you're an enterprise marketing organization, simultaneously changing the team structure, processes, and principles for every member of your department is a bad idea. Even the most experienced Agile coach can't predict exactly how a transformation will proceed in a new company, so you need to reduce the risk as much as possible in the face of this uncertainty.

The problem with the pilot concept, however, is that many marketing leaders misunderstand its aims and parameters. We pilot to reduce risk, but we also pilot to learn about how new processes and practices will (or won't) work in real life. The pilot, therefore, is only helpful if it represents the future state we want to reach. That future state includes persistent, dedicated, cross-functional, empowered teams, so that's what a pilot team needs to be.

Many marketing leaders want to reduce the risk by descoping the pilot efforts. Convinced that they can't fully devote people to a brand-new Rimarketing pilot team without disrupting the ongoing operations of the department, they try to have their proverbial cake and eat it too. Here's the usual line of reasoning:

1. Any fully functioning execution team needs a writer on it to be successful, so we definitely need a writer on our pilot.
2. Let's take a look at all our writers and see who might be a good fit.
3. Elizabeth is great, and she's excited to help work on these new processes, so let's have her join.
4. Elizabeth's manager Anica jumps in, fretting that Elizabeth is already involved in three big initiatives that won't be completed for another four months. What will happen to that work? The boss fears that her own department—the people she manages and whose performance is tied to her professional success—will suffer if Elizabeth gets pulled into a pilot.
5. At this point things often go awry. The other marketing leaders compromise by saying that Elizabeth will keep working on the existing three projects while she *also* joins the pilot.

Now, instead of emphasizing the focused effort that an execution team requires to succeed, we've brought in a team member who has conflicting priorities right from the start. Elizabeth also has a manager who's going to do her best to make sure that "her" work, not the work of the pilot, gets done first. Anica doesn't care about the pilot's success; she just wants to maintain control over her team. This is a recipe for failure.

Creating the right conditions for a fully dedicated pilot team is hard—sometimes extremely hard. But it's one of the most critical aspects of setting up your first execution team to succeed. Better to delay your pilot while you dial down someone's workload to free them up for full participation than to make piloting one more item on an already extensive to-do list.

In our hypothetical example, rather than compromise with Anica and agree to let Elizabeth take her current work with her to the pilot, that group needs to either (1) wait until Elizabeth's current projects are done and avoid giving her anything new in the meantime, or (2) transfer those projects to other writers to allow Elizabeth to focus on the pilot.

As you can see, your first job is to choose the pilot team carefully and ensure that they can be fully dedicated to the new team. The pilot will work on items from its queue and nothing else. Remember that we want all execution teams to have a meaningful, customer-centric reason to collaborate, and core KPIs that will be used to evaluate their success. That holds true for the pilot team as well. Don't just throw together a random collection of people with cross-functional skills and call it a pilot. Find a real reason for them to work together, and clarify how they'll be measured.

If you're struggling with what that "meaningful reason" might be, you may benefit from applying the Rimarketing principle of visibility. Get your marketing leadership together and create a list of everything you plan to work on in the next six months. Write all the projects down on a whiteboard or on some big pages posted on a wall, and look at the patterns. If there's a significant initiative that would benefit from a team's focused attention, that might be your pilot team's sole purpose for joining forces. Or maybe there's a collection of projects that share a theme. Maybe you're approaching conference season, and the pilot could focus on event marketing. Or maybe a particular business unit has a lot of demands coming your way, and you could funnel all that work to the pilot. Whatever shared purpose you decide on, you want to create a pilot execution team that has fully dedicated members as well as a clear idea of its mandate.

Once you've established who will be on your first execution team and how you'll evaluate its outcomes, two final steps will give your Rimarketing implementation its best chance of success. The first is to establish a performance baseline against which you can compare the team over time, and the second is to conduct a formal team kickoff meeting.

For the first step, it's ideal if you have preexisting data (e.g., releasing a campaign usually takes eight months; most projects require nine rounds of revisions; we produce a dozen pieces of content per month). But if you don't, let your new execution team run for a few weeks using whatever work-management methods currently exist in your marketing department (even if there aren't any). Don't make the team fully dedicated yet, don't start conducting daily standup meetings, and don't visualize their work. Just do things the way you normally would, and measure what happens. Then, after you make the switch to your new ways of working, you can accurately compare the pilot team's performance to some baseline metrics.

If you let the pilot carry on using traditional ways of working while you establish a baseline, wait to conduct the kickoff meeting until you're ready to fully transform the pilot group into a functioning execution team. This day-long session marks the start of an execution team's life. It establishes a formal beginning and helps launch the team into its journey. If you're uncertain how to execute a good kickoff, I highly recommend the book *Liftoff*, by Ainsley Nies and Diana Larsen. If you'd like a professional to facilitate it, my firm, AgileSherpas, conducts kickoffs for new teams.

During a kickoff, the execution team needs to complete several action items:

- **Write a working agreement.** How do we as a team want to behave with one another? What norms should we establish? What happens if someone violates our agreed-on code of conduct?
- **Visualize the workflow, a.k.a. build a kanban board.** This is most easily done with physical tools like whiteboards and sticky notes. If the team will be using a digital tool, they can transfer their physical sketch into the tool afterward.
- **Agree on initial WIP limits.** Will the team limit its work in progress by team member, by stages of the workflow, or with the board as a whole? It's time to make this tough call, knowing that it can be adjusted later on.

- **Establish when and where meetings will happen.** Colocated teams should pick a room and reserve it if needed. Distributed teams should decide how they'll all log in via video and what happens if someone can't attend. The team should share this information with others who might be interested in sitting in on their meetings.
- **Generate some buzz.** Team members may need to get to know one another, break the ice a little, or become excited about the work they're embarking on. Give them a fun activity to close out the day and mark the beginning of this great adventure.

An ideal length for an execution team pilot is between three and six months. This allows enough time for the team to gel and to work out any initial interpersonal challenges they might encounter. A few months should also allow them to accomplish substantial work that can be accurately compared to work generated by previous methods. That said, I don't suggest putting a hard stop date on your pilot. Give them the three- to six-month window, and see when a natural pause happens. If you shut it down right at three months no matter what, you may demoralize a team that was just building momentum. Likewise, if they finish their projects at four months but you force them to continue for another two, they may struggle to find meaning in their work. Set a range, and keep your leadership in touch with the pilot team so everyone can agree on a useful stopping point.

A final word about running pilots: having a single team attempting to radically alter the way they work can be one of the most challenging moments of a Rimarketing implementation. No other groups exist to support the fledgling execution team, and if they have dependencies on other, non-Agile teams, they almost certainly will encounter bottlenecks. For all these reasons and more, I strongly recommend enlisting coaching support during the pilot phase. It eliminates some of the isolation experienced by pilot teams, and it facilitates process iterations that will be crucial for scaling efforts.

Furthermore, conflicts will almost inevitably arise during the pilot phase. They may be among the team members, with external partners, or with marketing leadership. Conflict isn't bad, and in fact it's one of the reasons pilots are so valuable. You can reveal and resolve issues with a single team rather than during a multiteam, scaled rollout.

Scaling Marketing Agility

If you're a smallish marketing department, you may just need to kick off a couple of execution teams and get on with doing outstanding work. But groups of forty and up need to consider the challenge of scaling. Every flaw in a system becomes magnified when the system grows, so it's vital to "nail it before you scale it," as my fellow Agile coaches would say. In other words, use the pilot approach to work out the kinks *before* you roll out Rimarketing to an entire marketing organization. The counterbalancing principle to this idea comes in the form of another saying from the Agile community: "perfect is the enemy of done."

When attempting a scaled implementation of marketing agility, commonly known as an Agile transformation, you need to balance perfecting the process with a rapid rollout. Yes, you need to learn as much as possible during the pilot phase so that future teams succeed more quickly. But you cannot drag out piloting for years on end. The initial excitement over the change wanes quickly and is usually replaced by impatience and skepticism. Remember that your timeline for making the switch is finite. You've got four scaling steps to complete, and you should aim to do so in eighteen to twenty-four months max:

1. **Build the mindset.** Make the case for the change. Why should leaders, individual contributors, and external partners or stakeholders get on board? Document your "why" and the principles that you'll build on to get there. You may use Rimarketing principles, more standard Agile principles, or your own custom list. But you need strong shared understanding across all groups to give your future efforts the best chance of success.
2. **Test and evolve practices.** Here's where pilots come in. The composition of your pilot teams should be public

knowledge, as should the ways they'll be measured. If you have regular all-hands meetings, let the pilot team report on its progress, as well as on how it's iterating on Rimarketing practices.

3. **Draft a scaling plan.** As early as possible, create a plan outlining which teams will follow the pilot and approximately when. Hold true to the Rimarketing value of a bias toward action, and avoid waiting too long before spinning up new teams. The scaling plan should be public knowledge, as should any adjustments it undergoes based on feedback from existing execution teams or strategy groups.
4. **Scale intelligently.** Continue tracking both process- and team-level metrics as you grow the number of teams. Be prepared to learn new things about team structures, interpersonal dynamics, and collaborations with other departments. Respond to change rather than blindly following your plan.

Rimarketing is designed to be a modular framework, meaning you can easily add more execution teams and strategy groups over time. Your leadership team should already exist, although you may need to expand it slightly to include nonmarketing leadership. You may not need a true strategy group for your first pilot execution team, but as soon as you have two or more execution teams, your strategy group should also be set. Then it's simply a matter of adding more gears to the machine as you go.

Let's take a look at how two organizations approached their transformations.

Rimarketing in an Imperfect World

A fast-moving consumer-goods company was being disrupted by new consumer trends and habits. The executive leadership recognized that all facets of the organization needed to take a different approach to getting things done if they were going to keep up. They undertook a complete Agile transformation across the enterprise.

Like many organizations in a similar situation, they retained one of the big consulting companies to help manage this change. The consultants did their thing, eventually drafting a massive series of PowerPoint decks to guide the process. All seemed to be proceeding well, until the senior vice president of marketing, we'll call him Sven, saw the plan for how his department would be folded into the larger transformation effort. His instincts instantly told him it was way off base.

The marketing department was already centered around several brands, each of which needed to support the sale of its particular products across multiple global regions. In the current system, marketing leaders came up with the strategy for the products and brands, which the different teams would execute. But every region within the brands had its own nuances. Cultural differences have an impact on marketing preferences and buying behavior, and they had to be accounted for, as did local regulations on their industry. By the time marketing material actually made it to a consumer, it might be very different from the original strategic vision of leadership.

In addition, the hierarchical structure meant that the people setting strategy were far removed from the outcomes of the marketing campaigns. There were executive marketing leaders, regional leaders, brand-specific strategists, functional managers, and agencies doing much of the work, and the connection points among different groups were sparse. As happens in many large, global marketing organizations, unnecessary rework, little collaboration, and inconsistent messaging were common, all due to high levels of distribution and low levels of connection.

Given this complexity, Sven was worried. The new Agile plan featured a similar structure, with brand-centric teams under a vice president. The main difference was that outside of a small group of directors and managers, most of the marketing employees would be in an "Agile pool." They would float to different project teams based on the work needed at any given time. The hope was that no Agile pool member would be on more than three project teams simultaneously, but they might also be pulled into larger cross-functional teams at the organizational level to provide marketing expertise. Sven lacked confidence in this arrangement, but having never participated in an Agile transformation, he was unsure exactly what to propose as an alternative. A more marketing-specific approach to agility was needed, so AgileSherpas got involved.

I share this story here because this large department is messy. It doesn't line up perfectly with the Rimarketing framework—few groups ever do—and yet the framework still holds up. The hardest part was looking at their current headcount and making it work with a more Agile, less hierarchical arrangement. Our main objective was to find a way to create stable, persistent teams that had a chance at performing well. If the majority of every team was made up of folks from the Agile pool, all of whom sat on several teams and moved around every few weeks, meeting that goal was impossible. We couldn't get away from the Agile pool entirely, because the group lacked enough people with the right skills to create purely persistent teams.

We worked out a compromise. The Agile pool was distributed during quarterly big-room planning, and its members would remain with a persistent brand team for at least that quarter. If anyone from the pool absolutely had to sit on two different teams, those two teams should be within the same pack to reduce coordination efforts and context switching as much as possible.

The final story I want to share is of another transformation that at first glance lines up imperfectly with the Rimarketing framework. A financial services firm had gone through a reorganization within the past year, so although they wanted to adopt Agile ways of working, they were unwilling to create new cross-functional teams that would disrupt the org chart yet again.

Using Rimarketing principles for organizational design, we simply created persistent execution teams based on function (digital, public relations, internal communications, etc.), centered around a strategy group for each division. Individual contributors still enjoy a reduction in context switching and increased time for focused work. And through effective use of scaled daily standup meetings, the execution teams benefit from greater collaboration and communication, all without traditional Agile cross-functional teams.

These two examples demonstrate that there's no good excuse to reject a chance to improve your processes. Through creative thinking (and a strong understanding of the principles behind stable, persistent, Agile teams), you can create a structure that delivers the benefits of agility. And since Rimarketing is a modular framework, you can begin with a pilot team and steadily add more execution teams over time.

Getting from Here to There

Of course, with large marketing organizations it's never a good idea to take everyone through a transformation simultaneously. Piloting before jumping into the Agile deep end is key. In both the above examples, a few execution teams adopted new processes first, documented their efforts, and laid the groundwork for future teams. Even though only a couple of teams changed their ways initially, every member of both organizations went through foundational training early in the transformation. This approach allows new teams to rapidly spin up whenever the time is right, rather than waiting until everyone can get together *again* to conduct another series of workshops. See Figure 29 for an illustration of how a rollout might proceed.

You'll notice that all the new teams aim to be up and running within a year of the initial pilot effort. The relatively quick turnaround is why joint up-front training works. Department-wide training is less effective if a year and a half passes before everyone is fully Agile. Promoting a tight rollout schedule is a major consideration from a change-management perspective too. Yes, getting hundreds of people to fundamentally alter the way they do their work is a big undertaking (it's not called "transformation" for nothing). But if you drag your pilot efforts out for two years, fail to socialize the results, and don't document your plans for an eventual rollout, you're setting yourself up for failure.

People get fatigued with the whole transformation thing within about a year. If major progress hasn't occurred, they suspect that nothing will *really* happen, which gives them tacit permission not to buy in to the change. And when faced with the choice to change or stick with the status quo, most people will choose the status quo every time.

Don't let complexity and uncertainty keep you from making strides. Every marketing department in the world is complex. Nobody is certain about how the end of their transformation will look.

FIGURE 29

Rimarketing Pilot and Rollout Phases

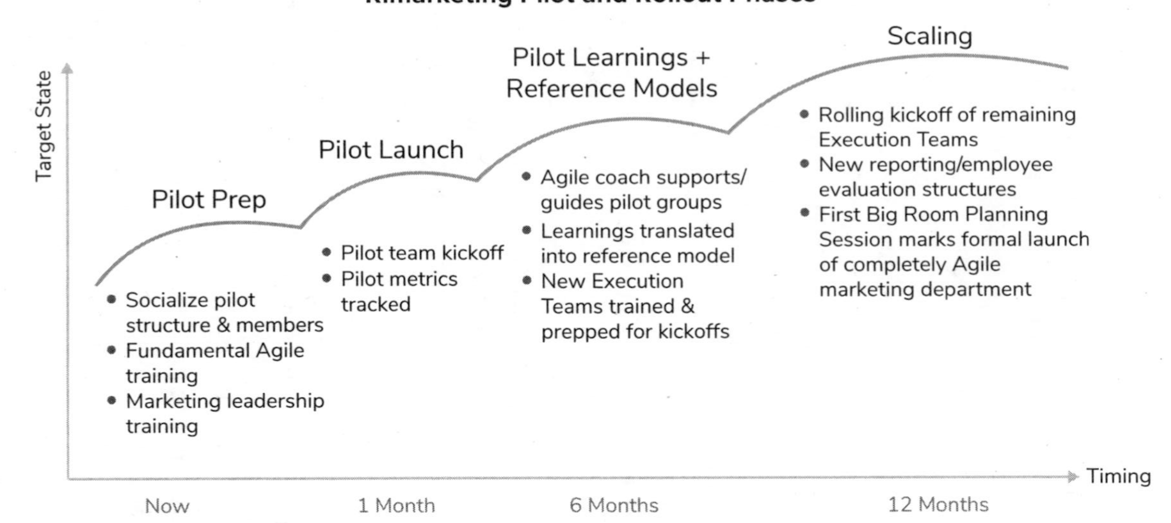

Rimarketing Framework® AgileSherpas

The groups that successfully transition from a current broken state to an Agile world of high performance are those that move forward anyway. If you're unsure how to do that, give me a shout and I can help. You can also follow this roadmap:

- **Stage 1: Pilot.** Put together your first wave of marketing agility. As discussed, make sure you document the team's work, free them to commit 100 percent to this effort, and ensure that everyone has visibility around how things are going.
- **Stage 2: Leadership Training.** Begin an Agile leader is different from being a traditional one. Set your transformation up for success by giving your marketing leadership the tools they need. Don't expect that they'll magically understand how to make the change happen.
- **Stage 3: Support and Repeat.** Once you've got some pilot work under your belt, create a reference model for the next teams. Document what works, what to avoid, how to start strong, etc. If needed, enterprise teams can create a separate executive action team, a group of leaders responsible for overseeing the transformation's success.
- **Stage 4: Scale and Socialize.** As more teams spin up, share their learnings and discuss the plan for the final transition. Avoid transformation burnout by providing a window for completion. In the spirit of radical transparency, socialize everything that happens around the transformation.
- **Stage 5: Assess and Evolve.** Keep an eye on both process and marketing metrics so you can correct course as needed. Be prepared to get some things wrong, and evolve your practices accordingly. Embrace failure as part of the process.
- **Stage 6: New Hires.** Don't assume that everyone you interview will automatically understand agility. Be clear about how they're expected to work in your new Rimarketing world. This goes for individual contributors all the way up to executives. Nothing destroys a hard-won transformation faster than an unsupportive new leader.

I've visualized these stages in a linear way mostly to accommodate how we humans like to view information. Several of these stages will occur simultaneously, and you may find yourself returning to previous stages as you progress on the larger journey. Don't worry too much about the order; just ensure that you hit all the checkpoints.

CONCLUSION

Although I've provided some anecdotes from my coaching experience, you may have noticed that this book is light on what might be called "case studies." This isn't because case studies don't exist; it's to save us from ourselves. Marketers love us some case studies. We want to know that teams like ours with similar challenges and idiosyncrasies have managed to achieve the goal we've set for ourselves. It's comforting and comfortable to have those examples laid out for us.

But case studies too often become crutches and excuses. If they exist for an industry or team like ours, we mindlessly copy and paste their steps. If they don't exist, we use their absence as an excuse for inaction.

Neither of these paths is in keeping with the Shu Ha Ri approach that forms the foundation of this book, so I've deliberately avoided including case studies. My hope is that you'll be sufficiently excited about the potential of agility (or sufficiently annoyed with the problems in your current processes) to embrace the principles, processes, and practices of Rimarketing, case study or no.

As you consider your own path up the mountain of marketing agility, I hope you'll find the Rimarketing framework a valuable guide. It's the product of years of hands-on training with hundreds of marketers in dozens of organizations, and it will serve you well in your transformation efforts.

But they will, in the end, be your own efforts.

Kazuo Chiba, the world-renowned martial arts master whose quotation opens Part Five, has spoken eloquently about the Shu Ha Ri cycle and mastery in general. He realizes that he "can't simply give or transfer my budo [martial arts expertise] to my students. At most I can invite them into my experience to have them use it as a guide to completing their own budo." Everyone's journey is unique, "because you can't learn, lock-stock-and-barrel, what your teacher has achieved." I've tried to outline the paths that have worked for me and my clients, but I've realized, like Chiba, that every transformation has its own flavor. Its individual character "simply won't emerge for you in exactly the same form as [it] did for your teacher."[1]

You can use stories as signposts—for either the paths to take or the paths to avoid—but not even the detailed framework I've laid out in this book can tell you everything you need to know. Embrace the bias for action and take your first steps. Then, in the spirit of Rimarketing and the Shu Ha Ri tradition, be prepared to ri-think, ri-work, and ri-evaluate.

Your journey toward true mastery of marketing agility starts now.

---

1. Josh Gold, "Interview with Kazuo Chiba," *Aikido Journal*, April 26, 2004, https://aikidojournal.com/2004/04/26/interview-with-kazuo-chiba-1/.

Acknowledgments

First billing, in this and all things, must go to Dan Partain, my amazing partner in life as well as the creator of the graphics for this book. From uncomplaining weeks of solo parenting while I was on-site with clients to giving invaluable feedback on the user experience of this book, you've done more than anyone to support me. You're the best.

Much love and appreciation to my kids, Brennan and Caroline, who somehow understand that even though she gets on a plane a lot, their mom still loves them beyond words.

Many thanks to Berrett-Koehler and my awesome editor, Charlotte Ashlock, who made my first experience with traditional publishing a great one. I so appreciate your belief in marketing agility and its power to transform the professional lives of marketers everywhere.

Major high fives to my partners at AgileSherpas, Peter Martin and Raviv Turner. Thank you for listening to early ramblings about the Rimarketing framework, and for helping me apply it to our clients' organizations. Thank you also for pushing me to clarify aspects of my thinking, so people outside my brain could follow these ideas.

To all of AgileSherpas' clients, past, present, and future, thank you from the bottom of my heart for trusting us to guide you toward greater marketing agility. The past few years have been the most rewarding of my professional career, and you are the reason.

Index

Page numbers followed by "f" indicate figures; page numbers followed by "t" indicate tables.

About the Author

Photo by Andrea Fryrear

Andrea Fryrear is cofounder, partner, and Agile marketing coach at AgileSherpas, the world's leading Agile marketing training and consulting group. She spends the majority of her time helping marketing organizations, from global Fortune 50 enterprises to scrappy startups, transform their operations by applying Agile principles and practices. Andrea is also a highly sought-after international keynote speaker; her recent appearances include Content Marketing World, MarTech, Conex, and Dialogkonferansen, to name just a few.

Andrea is coauthor of the world's first internationally recognized Agile marketing certification, which is accredited through the International Consortium for Agile (ICAgile). She holds a wide range of Agile certifications, including Certified Scrum Master (CSM), Advanced Certified Product Owner (A-CSPO), Certified Professional in Agile Coaching (ICP-ACC), Certified Scrum@Scale Practitioner, Certified Agile Leader (CAL-1), Certified Professional in Agile Marketing (ICP-MKG), and ICAgile Authorized Instructor.

In addition to *Mastering Marketing Agility*, Andrea is the author of *Death of a Marketer* (Corsac), which chronicles marketing's troubled past and charts a course to its more Agile future.

On the rare occasions when she's not on a stage or with a client, Andrea can be found in her adopted home of Boulder, Colorado, where she lives with her husband and two kids.

Berrett–Koehler Publishers

Berrett-Koehler is an independent publisher dedicated to an ambitious mission: *Connecting people and ideas to create a world that works for all.*

Our publications span many formats, including print, digital, audio, and video. We also offer online resources, training, and gatherings. And we will continue expanding our products and services to advance our mission.

We believe that the solutions to the world's problems will come from all of us, working at all levels: in our society, in our organizations, and in our own lives. Our publications and resources offer pathways to creating a more just, equitable, and sustainable society. They help people make their organizations more humane, democratic, diverse, and effective (and we don't think there's any contradiction there). And they guide people in creating positive change in their own lives and aligning their personal practices with their aspirations for a better world.

And we strive to practice what we preach through what we call "The BK Way." At the core of this approach is *stewardship,* a deep sense of responsibility to administer the company for the benefit of all of our stakeholder groups, including authors, customers, employees, investors, service providers, sales partners, and the communities and environment around us. Everything we do is built around stewardship and our other core values of *quality, partnership, inclusion,* and *sustainability.*

This is why Berrett-Koehler is the first book publishing company to be both a B Corporation (a rigorous certification) and a benefit corporation (a for-profit legal status), which together require us to adhere to the highest standards for corporate, social, and environmental performance. And it is why we have instituted many pioneering practices (which you can learn about at www.bkconnection.com), including the Berrett-Koehler Constitution, the Bill of Rights and Responsibilities for BK Authors, and our unique Author Days.

We are grateful to our readers, authors, and other friends who are supporting our mission. We ask you to share with us examples of how BK publications and resources are making a difference in your lives, organizations, and communities at www.bkconnection.com/impact.

Dear reader,

Thank you for picking up this book and welcome to the worldwide BK community! You're joining a special group of people who have come together to create positive change in their lives, organizations, and communities.

What's BK all about?

Our mission is to connect people and ideas to create a world that works for all.

Why? Our communities, organizations, and lives get bogged down by old paradigms of self-interest, exclusion, hierarchy, and privilege. But we believe that can change. That's why we seek the leading experts on these challenges—and share their actionable ideas with you.

A welcome gift

To help you get started, we'd like to offer you a **free copy** of one of our bestselling ebooks:

www.bkconnection.com/welcome

When you claim your **free ebook**, you'll also be subscribed to our blog.

Our freshest insights

Access the best new tools and ideas for leaders at all levels on our blog at ideas.bkconnection.com.

Sincerely,

Your friends at Berrett-Koehler